Rick Ste

PO

ITALY'S CINQUE TERRE

Rick Steves

Contents

Introduction

Tucked between Genoa and Pisa, in a mountainous and seductive corner of the Italian Riviera, lies the Cinque Terre (CHINK-weh TAY-reh)—five villages carving a good life out of difficult terrain. With a traffic-free charm—a happy result of natural isolation—the Cinque Terre offers a rugged alternative to the glitzy Riviera resorts nearby.

Each village fills a ravine with a lazy hive of human activity. Calloused locals and sunburned travelers enjoy the area's unique mix of Italian culture and nature. There isn't a Fiat or museum in sight—just sun, sea, sand (well, pebbles), wine, and pure, unadulterated Italy. Choose a home base according to just how cut off you'd like to be from the outer world: resorty

The Cinque Terre at a Glance

The Cinque Terre

▲▲**Monterosso al Mare** Resorty, flat, and spread out along the coast, with a charming old town, a modern new town, and the Cinque Terre's best beaches, swimming, and nightlife. See page 37.

▲▲**Vernazza** The region's gem—the most touristy and dramatic—crowned with a ruined castle above and a lively harborfront cradling a natural harbor below. See page 59.

▲**Corniglia** Quiet hilltop village known for its cooler temperatures (it's the only one of the five villages set above the water), fewer tourists, and a tradition of fine wines. See page 87.

▲▲**Manarola** Mellow, hiking-focused waterfront village wrapped in vineyards and dotted with a picturesque mix of shops and cliff-climbing houses. See page 95.

▲**Riomaggiore** The most workaday of the five villages, with nightlife, too. See page 109.

Near the Cinque Terre

Levanto Town popular with surfers for its long beach; has speedy train connections to the Cinque Terre, and is a short walk from ▲**Bonassola,** a sleepy, scenic beach village. See page 125.

▲**Sestri Levante** Charming town on a peninsula flanked by two crescent beaches. See page 135.

▲▲**Santa Margherita Ligure** Easygoing old-school resort town with an enjoyable urban bustle, a handful of sights, and close proximity to Portofino. See page 141.

▲**Portofino** Yacht-harbor resort with grand scenery and easy connections (by boat, bus, or foot) from Santa Margherita Ligure. See page 152.

▲▲**Porto Venere** Enchanting seafront village perfect for a scenic side-trip by boat from the Cinque Terre or by bus from La Spezia. See page 158.

La Spezia Beachless transportation hub, with trains to the Cinque Terre and a bus to Porto Venere. See page 162.

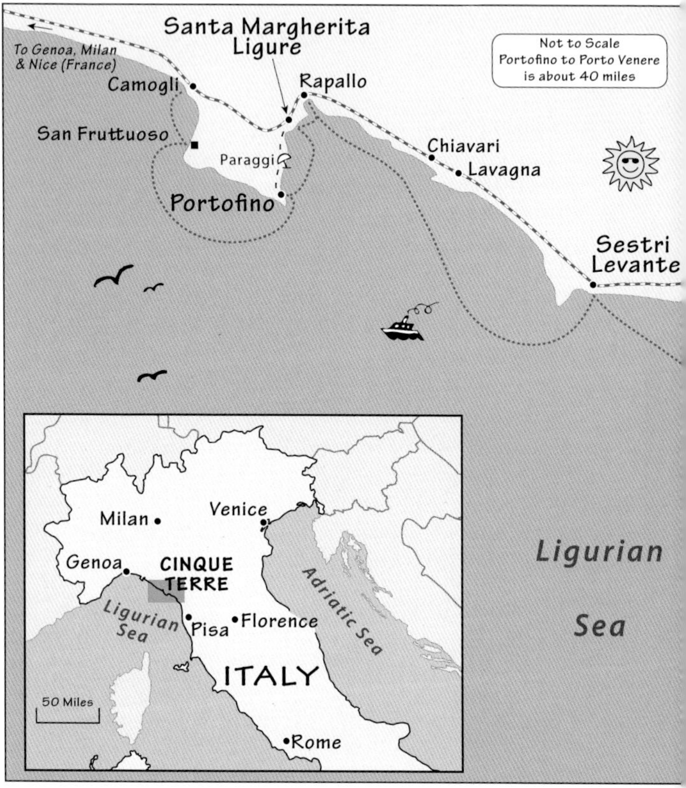

Monterosso, cover-girl Vernazza, hilltop Corniglia, photogenic Manarola, and amiable Riomaggiore.

The Cinque Terre is my kind of perfect, but these nearby resort towns are tempting: Levanto, Sestri Levante, Santa Margherita Ligure, and Portofino to the north, and Porto Venere to the south, anchored by a major transit hub, La Spezia.

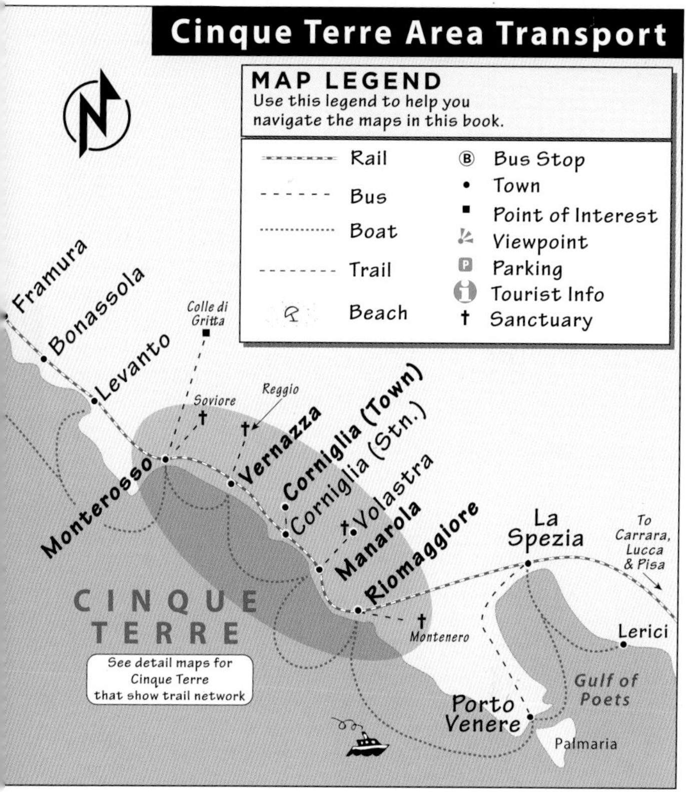

Planning Your Time

The ideal stay in the Cinque Terre is two or three full days; my recommended minimum stay is two nights and an uninterrupted day. Be warned: The Cinque Terre has a strange way of messing up your momentum. Staying for too short a time would be a mistake you'd likely regret.

The villages are connected by trains, boats, and trails. There's no checklist of sights or experiences—just a hike, the towns themselves,

Key to this Book

Abbreviations and Times

Tourist information offices are abbreviated as **TI,** and bathrooms are **WCs.**

Like Europe, this book uses the **24-hour clock.** It's the same through 12:00 noon, then keeps going: 13:00, 14:00, and so on. For anything over 12, subtract 12 and add P.M. (14:00 is 2:00 P.M.).

When giving **opening times,** I include both peak season and off-season hours if they differ. So, if a sight is listed as "May-Oct daily 9:00-16:00," it should be open from 9 A.M. until 4 P.M. from the first day of May until the last day of October (but expect exceptions).

For **transit** or **tour departures,** I first list the frequency, then the duration. So a train connection listed as "2/hour, 1.5 hours" departs twice each hour, and the journey lasts an hour and a half.

Sights and Experiences

These are rated:

▲▲▲	Don't miss
▲▲	Try hard to see
▲	Worthwhile if you can make it
No rating	Worth knowing about

Accommodations

These are classified based on the average price of a standard double room with breakfast in high season:

$$$$	**Splurge:** Most rooms are €170 or more.
$$$	**Pricier:** €130–170
$$	**Moderate:** €90–130
$	**Budget:** €50–90
¢	**Backpacker:** Under €50
RS%	**Rick Steves discount**

Unless otherwise noted, credit cards are accepted, hotel staff speak basic English, and Wi-Fi is free. For the best deal, *book directly with the hotel.* Ask for a discount if paying in cash or if the listing includes RS%.

Restaurants

These are classified based on the average cost of a typical main course (pasta or *secondi*—second course):

$$$$	**Splurge:** Most main courses over €20
$$$	**Pricier:** €15–20
$$	**Moderate:** €10–15
$	**Budget:** Under €10

Drinks, desserts, and splurge items (steak and seafood) can raise the price considerably. In Italy, pizza by the slice and other takeout food is **$;** a basic trattoria or sit-down pizzeria is **$$;** a casual but more upscale restaurant is **$$$;** and a swanky splurge is **$$$$.**

and your fondest vacation desires. Study this book in advance to piece together your best visit, mixing hiking, swimming, trains, and boat rides.

You could spend one day hiking from town to town (taking a boat or train part of the way, or as the return trip). Spend a second day visiting any towns you've yet to see, comparing main streets, beaches, and focaccia.

Here's a sample day: If you're based in Monterosso, take a morning train to Corniglia, hike to Vernazza for lunch (where you could explore the town, hike to the grand-view cemetery, or cool off at the beach), then catch the boat to Monterosso to stroll the beach promenade. And that's only one day out of dozens of memorable Cinque Terre combinations you can dream up.

On any evening, linger over dinner, enjoy live music at a low-key club (or summer opera in Vernazza!), try a wine tasting, or follow one of my self-guided town walks. At sunset, take a glass of your favorite beverage out to the breakwater to watch the sun slip into the Mediterranean.

With extra time, visit the towns near the Cinque Terre. If you carve out a day and an overnight for Santa Margherita Ligure, fit in an

afternoon side-trip to Portofino. A day trip to Levanto (by train or a hike from Monterosso) with an excursion to Bonassola's beach is fun. (Some travelers flip-flop this by staying in Levanto and day-tripping to the Cinque Terre.) For double the beaches, visit Sestri Levante. South of the Cinque Terre, lovely Porto Venere merits a day trip.

Market days perk up the Cinque Terre and nearby towns from around 8:00 to 13:00 on Tuesday in Vernazza, Wednesday in Levanto, Thursday in Monterosso, Friday in La Spezia and Santa Margherita Ligure, and Saturday in Sestri Levante.

Trip Tips: Make a point to get the most out of the cool, relaxed, and quiet hours early and late in the day (great times to start a coastal hike), to help you avoid the worst crowds. The vast majority of visitors to the Cinque Terre are day-trippers. Between 10:00 and 15:00—especially on weekends—masses of gawkers unload from boats, tour buses, and cruise ships, inundating the villages and changing the feel of the region. For more advice on beating the crowds, see page 20.

Finally, make time to wander, shop, and simply be. Stop often for gelato. Write a poem over a glass of local wine in a sun-splashed, wave-dashed village. Be open to unexpected experiences and the friendliness of the local people. As you visit places I know and love, I'm happy you'll be meeting some of my favorite Italians.

Happy travels! *Buon viaggio!*

The Cinque Terre

This breathtakingly scenic chunk of coast was first described in medieval times as the "five lands" *(cinque terre).* Tiny communities grew up in the shadows of castles—lookouts for pirate raids. As the threat of pirates faded, the villages prospered, catching fish and cultivating grapes. But until the advent of tourism in this generation, the towns remained isolated. Even today, each village comes with its own traditions, a distinct dialect, and a proud heritage. Say the towns' poetic names with an Italian accent: Monterosso, Vernazza (ver-NAHT-sah), Corniglia (cor-NEEL-yah), Manarola (mah-nah-ROH-lah), and Riomaggiore (ree-oh-mah-JOR-ay).

The Cinque Terre is now a national park, where all can enjoy the villages, hiking, swimming, boat rides, and evening romance of one of

God's great gifts to tourism. While the region is now well-discovered and can get jam-packed, I've never seen happier, more relaxed tourists.

ORIENTATION

This chapter focuses on how to navigate the Cinque Terre, using a mix of trains, boats, and hikes. Chapters on each of the towns follow, with all the specifics you need for your visit. For tips on eating in Italy (including local specialties), accommodations, using mobile devices, and more, see the Practicalities chapter.

Tourist and Park Information

Each town's train station has a Cinque Terre National Marine Park information office, which generally also serves as an all-purpose town TI and gift shop. They can usually answer questions about trails (including closures), shuttle bus schedules, and so on (www.parconazionale5terre.it). For more on the region, see www.cinqueterre.it.

Useful Blogs: CinqueTerreInsider.com, written by a resident American expat, is filled with up-to-date practicalities for visitors to this always-in-flux region. Another good site, run by caring locals, is **Visit Vernazza** (www.visitvernazza.org).

Arrival in the Cinque Terre

By Train

The five towns of the Cinque Terre are on a milk-run line, with trains coming through about every 30 minutes, and connecting with La Spezia and Levanto.

Most big, fast trains speed right past the Cinque Terre, although a few IC trains connect Monterosso to Milan or Pisa. Unless you're coming from another Cinque Terre town, you'll have to change trains at least once to reach Manarola, Corniglia, or Vernazza. Coming from the south or east, you'll probably transfer at La Spezia's Centrale station (not La Spezia Migliarina); see page 164. Coming from the north, you'll transfer at Monterosso (see page 57), Levanto, Sestri Levante, or Genoa's Piazza Principe station. Local train info tel. 0187-817-458, www.trenitalia.com.

By Car

Given the narrow roads, I wouldn't bring a car to the Cinque Terre; you won't need it, and parking can be a headache. But if your plans require a car, try to stay at a hotel with parking; Monterosso is your best bet (and also has parking lots in town). It's smart to have your hotel confirmation in hand during busy times—holidays, summer, and weekends—when police at the top of town may deny entry to cars without a hotel reservation.

Each Cinque Terre town has a parking lot (great for day-trippers and overnighters) on its outskirts, with a shuttle bus into town. The rare street parking in the towns is best left for locals. Wherever you park, leave nothing of value in your car.

To reach **Monterosso** from A-12, take the Carrodano-Levanto exit (see page 38 for specifics). Don't drive to **Vernazza:** The road is in poor condition and parking is scarce; it's better to park in Levanto or La Spezia and ride the train in. For **Riomaggiore, Corniglia,** or **Manarola,** leave the freeway at La Spezia and follow the road that parallels the coast (with access to each town except Monterosso).

Helpful Hints

Pickpocket Alert: At peak times, the Cinque Terre can be notoriously crowded, and pickpockets aggressively and expertly work the most congested areas. Be on guard, especially in train stations, on platforms, and while you're on trains and boats, particularly when getting on or off with a crush of people. Wear a money belt, and keep your things zipped up and buttoned down.

Money: You'll find ATMs and banks throughout the region.

Tours and Activities: Arbaspàa, based in Manarola, sets up wine tastings, cooking classes, fishing trips, and more (www.arbaspaa.com; see page 104). **Cinque Terre Riviera,** based in Vernazza, books vacation rentals throughout the region, Vernazza opera tickets, cooking classes, and more (www.cinqueterreriviera.com; see page 61). **BeautifuLiguria,** run by Anna Merulla, offers various excursions (www.beautifuliguria.com).

Local Guides: Andrea Bordigoni is knowledgeable and a delight (€125/half-day, €210/day, mobile 393-133-9409, bordigo@inwind.it). Other guides are **Marco Brizzi** (mobile 328-694-2847, www.hi-ke.com, marco_brizzi@yahoo.it) and **Paola Tommarchi** (paolatomma@alice.it).

Rainy Day Activities: Explore the towns, taking trains to connect them; splurge for a tasty meal; or nurse a coffee or drink at a harborfront café while watching the roiling waves. If you hike, avoid the steeper trails in the rain; rocks can be slippery.

Wi-Fi: All Cinque Terre train stations offer free Wi-Fi with a Cinque Terre park card (see page 23). Many cafés and bars offer free Wi-Fi to customers.

Baggage Storage: You can pay to store bags at or near the train stations in Monterosso, Vernazza, and Riomaggiore (and at these towns near the Cinque Terre—La Spezia and Santa Margherita Ligure); see specifics per destination.

Services: Every train station has a free WC, but it's smart to bring your own toilet paper.

Taxi: Cinqueterre Taxi covers all five towns (mobile 334-776-1946 or 347-652-0837, www.cinqueterretaxi.com). The pricey **5 Terre Transfer** service can come in handy if you need to connect the five towns or beyond (Luciana mobile 339-130-1183; Marzio mobile 340-356-5268).

Getting Around the Cinque Terre

Within the Cinque Terre, you can connect towns in three ways: by train, boat, or foot. **Trains** are the cheapest, fastest, and most frequent option. But don't get stuck in a train rut: In calm weather, **boats** connect the towns nearly as frequently—and with much better scenery. (If you're in a rush, take whichever form of transport is leaving first.) And **hiking** lets you enjoy more pasta.

By Train

By train, the five towns are just a few minutes apart.

Tickets: A train ride of any length between Cinque Terre towns costs a hefty €4 during peak times—whether you're hopping one town or four. (It's half-price after about 19:00 and before 8:30.) There may also be an all-day ticket (likely €10). You can buy tickets at train station windows or Cinque Terre park desks, but to save time in line, use the self-service machines. These have English instructions, provide schedule information, and accept US credit cards (and often also euros).

Be sure to validate your ticket before you board by stamping it in the green-and-white machines located on train platforms and in station passages. Conductors here are notorious for levying stiff fines on tourists riding with an unstamped ticket. You can buy several tickets at once and use them as you like, validating as you go. If you have a Eurail Pass, don't use up one of your valuable travel days on the relatively cheap Cinque Terre.

Schedules: In peak season, trains generally run about twice hourly in each direction, connecting all five towns. (There can be troublesome gaps after about 19:00—check the schedule in advance.) Since the train is the Cinque Terre's lifeline, shops, hotels, and restaurants often post the current schedule, and many hand out copies. Study the key carefully to know which departures are only for weekdays, Sundays, and so on. The most foolproof option is to stop by a train station and check the real-time TV monitors to see the next departure time.

Important Note: Any train stopping at Vernazza, Corniglia, or Manarola is going to all of the towns. Trains from Levanto, Monterosso,

Trains connect the towns; use the ticket machine to save time.

Riomaggiore, or La Spezia sometimes skip lesser stations, so confirm that the train will stop at the town you need.

At the Platform: Monitors in each station clearly show departure times in each direction (and, if they're late—*in ritardo*—how many minutes behind they are; *SOPP* means "cancelled"). On the monitors, northbound trains are marked for *(per)* Levanto, Genova, or Sestri Levante; southbound trains are marked for La Spezia. To be sure you get on the right train, it helps to know your train's number and final destination. Northbound trains use the tracks closest to the water; southbound trains use the tracks on the mountain side.

Assuming you're on vacation, accept the unpredictability of Cinque Terre trains. They're often late—unless you are, too, in which case they're on time. Relax while you wait. Buy an ice cream or cup of coffee at a station bar, and scout the platform you need in advance. This is easy in Monterosso, with its fine café-with-a-view on track #1 (northbound), and in Vernazza, where you can hang out at the Blue Marlin Bar with a prepaid drink and dash when the train pulls in.

Getting Off: Know your stop. As the train leaves the town just before your destination, go to the door and get ready to slip out before the mobs flood in. A word to the wise for novice tourists, who often miss their stop: The stations are small and the trains are long, so (especially in Vernazza) you might have to get off deep in a tunnel. Also, the doors don't open automatically—you may have to open the handle of the door yourself (push the green button, twist the black handle, or lift up the red one).

By Boat

From Easter through October, a daily boat service connects Monterosso, Vernazza, Manarola, Riomaggiore, Porto Venere, and beyond. Though

Swimming and Kayaking

Every coastal town has a beach—or, at least, a rocky place to swim. Monterosso has the Cinque Terre's biggest and sandiest beach, with umbrellas and beach-use fees (but any stretch of beach without umbrellas is free). Vernazza's main beach and new beach are tiny—better for sunning than swimming (some people swim in the deep water off the breakwater). Manarola and Riomaggiore have the worst beaches (no sand), but Manarola offers the best deep-water swimming. Levanto, just a few minutes' train ride past Monterosso, has big and broad beaches, with even better ones an easy bike ride away, in Bonassola. And Sestri Levante, farther north, has two beautiful beaches.

Wear your walking shoes and pack your swim gear. Several beaches have showers. Don't tote your white hotel towels; most hotels will provide beach towels (sometimes for a fee). Underwater sightseeing is full of fish. Sea urchins line the rocks, and sometimes jellyfish wash up on the pebbles, so water shoes are essential (shoes and goggles sold in local shops).

You can rent **kayaks** or **boats** in Monterosso and Riomaggiore (see listings per town). While experienced boaters have a blast here, if you're not comfortable navigating a tippy kayak, the Cinque Terre is probably not the place to start.

hey can be very crowded, these boats provide a scenic way to get from own to town.

In peaceful weather, boats can be more reliable than trains. But because he boats nose in and tourists have to gingerly disembark onto little more than a plank, even just a small chop can cancel some or all of the stops.

Crowd-Beating Tips

Italy's slice of traffic-free Riviera has been discovered, frustrating both locals and conscientious visitors. The most dramatic influx is created by groups—whether day-tripping tours or mobs of cruise-ship sightseers. Avoid the worst of the logjams by following these tips:

Time your visit carefully. The busiest months are May, June, and September; July and August are slightly less crowded, but packed on weekends. Shoulder season—April and October—can be ideal, with fewer crowds and cooler temperatures for hiking (although it can be too cold to swim). Avoid holiday weekends (Easter and Italian Liberation Day on April 25) that bring peak-season crowds.

Make the most of your time early and late. Cruisers and day-trippers start pouring into the Cinque Terre around 10:00 and typically head out between 15:00 and 18:00. Those midday hours are your time to hit the beach, discover a back-street bar to nurse a glass of *sciacchetrà,* or find a hike away from the main trails. At midday, the main coastal trail is a hot human traffic jam. Starting a hike at 8:00 or 16:00 is a joy.

Escape to less crowded trails, towns, and activities. Beyond the busy coastal trail, there are plenty of hikes where you'll scarcely see another tourist. Or, on very crowded days, simply leave the Cinque Terre altogether. If you want to hit the beach but Monterosso is a human parking lot, hop the train a few minutes to Levanto, rent a bike, and pedal on a level path to the delightful beach at Bonassola (described on page 130). Or, stick around the Cinque Terre but find something fun to do away from the crowds—such as a wine tasting or a massage.

Sleep in the Cinque Terre—not nearby. Levanto and La Spezia are close and well-connected by train, making them popular home bases. But it's easier to enjoy the Cinque Terre early and late—when it's quiet

Tickets: The ticket price depends on the length of the boat ride (€5 for a short hop, and up to €15 for a five-town, one-way ticket with stops). An all-day Cinque Terre pass costs €22. Another all-day boat pass for €30 extends to Porto Venere; for an extra €5, you can add a 40-minute scenic ride around three small islands (2/day). Buy tickets at the little stands at each town's harbor (tel. 0187-818-440).

and cool—if you're actually sleeping here, even if it means paying a premium for accommodations.

Be careful on crowded train platforms. At peak times, be cautious, stay well behind the yellow line, and be alert for pickpockets. Spread out to less crowded areas to wait.

Hire your own boat. If the regularly scheduled boats are jammed, consider hiring your own boat to zip you to the next town. Captains hang out at each town's harbor, offering one-way transfers to other towns and hour-long cruises (see below).

Schedules: Boat schedules are posted at docks, harbor bars, Cinque Terre park offices, and hotels (www.navigazionegolfodeipoeti.it). Boats depart Monterosso about hourly (10:30-18:00), stopping at the Cinque Terre towns (except Corniglia, the hill town) and ending up an hour later in Porto Venere. Boats from Porto Venere to Monterosso run 8:50-18:00.

Private Boats: To escape the crowds—or for a scenic splurge—hire

Shuttles link to parking and hikes; boats link the towns.

a captain to ferry you between towns. For example, at the harbor in Vernazza, you can pay €30-50 to hop to any other Cinque Terre town. If you split the cost among a few fellow travelers, it's more affordable. Or you can hire a captain for a tour of the region (figure €150/1 hour). Captains offer their services at the harbors in Monterosso, Vernazza, Manarola, and Riomaggiore (see specific listings in the Monterosso and Vernazza sections).

By Shuttle Bus

ATC shuttle buses (which locals call *pulmino*) connect each Cinque Terre town with its closest parking lot and various points in the hills (but they don't connect the five towns to each other). The one you're most likely to use runs between Corniglia's train station and its hilltop town center. Most rides cost €1.50 (€2.50 from driver), and are free with a Cinque Terre park card (see next page). Buy tickets and ask about bus schedules at park info offices or TIs, or check times posted at bus stops. But be aware that shuttle schedules change constantly: Confirm the details before planning your day around the bus. Note that shuttles may not run during midafternoon lunch breaks (about 12:30-15:00). As you board, it's smart to tell the driver where you want to go. Departures often coordinate with train arrival times.

Some shuttles go beyond the parking lots and high into the hills—often terminating at the town's sanctuary church. To soak in the scenery, you can ride up and hike down, or just ride both ways (30-45 minutes round-trip, covered by one ticket).

HIKING THE CINQUE TERRE

The five Cinque Terre towns are connected by good trails, marked with red-and-white paint, white arrows, and some signs (*sentiero* means trail). Expect a trail or two to be closed for repair. Most visitors stick to the main coastal trail that links the villages, but hardy hikers can sidestep the crowds by venturing onto one of the region's alternate routes. Although I've described the hikes in one direction, you can start at either end.

Cinque Terre Park Cards: Visitors hiking on the main coastal trail between Riomaggiore and Monterosso must buy a park card (good for one or two days, with an option covering trains). Note that cards aren't needed to hike on any other trails.

Cards can be purchased at train stations, TIs, and trailheads, and are valid until midnight on the expiration date (and include free Wi-Fi at train stations). Write your name on your card or risk a fine. Those under 18 or over 70 get a discount, as do families of four or more. The configuration and pricing of these cards is often in flux—the following details may change. For the latest, consult the park's website: www.parconazionale5terre.it.

The **Cinque Terre Trekking Card** costs €7.50 for one day of hiking or €14.50 for two days (covers trails and ATC shuttle buses, but not trains).

The **Cinque Terre Treno Multi-Service Card** covers what the Trekking Card does, including local trains connecting all Cinque Terre towns, plus Levanto and La Spezia (€16/1 day, €29/2 days, validate card at train station by punching it in the machine). To break even with this card, you'd have to hike and take two train trips every day.

Trail Closures: Trails can be closed in bad weather or due to

Signs, markers, and arrows help guide hikers on trails.

Hikes at a Glance

Hikes can be done in either direction. Get local advice before you set out.

The Main Coastal Trail (Riomaggiore-Monterosso)

▲▲▲**Riomaggiore-Manarola** (Via dell'Amore; likely closed but may reopen soon) Easy, 20-minute, romantic stroll just above the water on a well-tended, level path.

Alternative Route: ▲ Riomaggiore-Manarola via "La Beccara" Challenging, 1.5-hour trail traversing mostly stone steps. Park card not required.

▲**Manarola-Corniglia** (likely closed) Scenic, moderately easy 45-minute hike just above the train tracks and coastline, but often closed due to landslide threat.

Alternative Route: ▲▲ Manarola-Corniglia via Volastra Demanding but gorgeous 2.5 hour hike through vineyards high over the coast; made much easier if you take the shuttle bus from Manarola to Volastra. Park card not required for hike, though it covers the cheap bus ride.

▲▲▲**Corniglia-Vernazza** Most scenic and rewarding stretch (1.5 hours) of the main coastal trail, with fine views, significant elevation changes, and moderately challenging stretches on uneven stone steps.

▲▲**Vernazza-Monterosso** Challenging but dramatic 1.5-hour hike, including long stretches of steep steps above Monterosso.

Extending the Coastal Trail

To the North

▲**Monterosso-Levanto** Logical northward continuation of the main coastal trail, a 3-hour hike over Punta Mesco; a notch more challenging than the rest of the coastal trail.

landslides. Before planning your hiking day, confirm whether any trail segments are closed. Official closures are noted on the national park website and are posted at the park-information desks in each town's train station. Some trails are closed because they are impassable, while a few are technically closed, but still hikable, at your own risk. Ask locals

▲**Levanto-Bonassola Promenade** Level rails-to-trails 30-minute hike that cuts through mountains (largely through tunnels) to connect Levanto to the beach town of Bonassola; fine by foot but better by bike.

To the South

▲**Riomaggiore-Porto Venere** Very demanding, 5-hour trek high into the hills, ending at picturesque Porto Venere.

High Route Between Porto Venere and Levanto

▲▲**Trail #1** Remote, cliff-capping 22-mile "Red Trail" high above the main coastal trail and the sanctuary trails, best for well-equipped, hardy hikers.

or fellow hikers for the latest on which trails are actually passable, but err on the side of caution.

Hiking Conditions: Other than the wide, easy Riomaggiore-Manarola segment, the main coastal trail is generally narrow, steep, rocky, and comes with lots of challenging steps. Don't overestimate your hiking abilities. I get

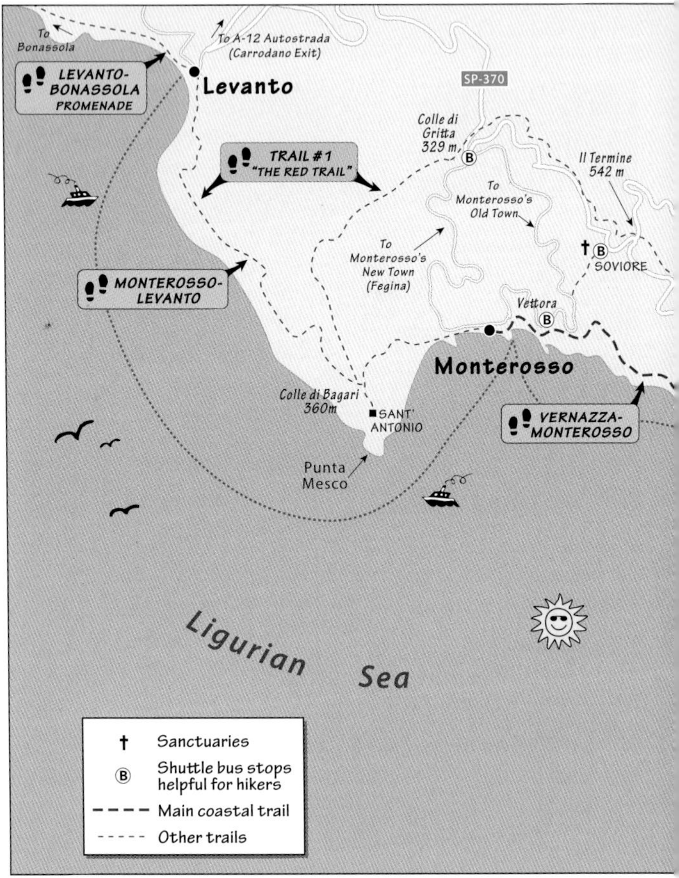

many emails from readers who say the trail was tougher than they'd expected. The rocks and metal grates can be slippery in the rain (I'd avoid the very steep Monterosso-Vernazza stretch if it's wet). Don't venture up on these rocky cliffs without sun protection (and/or a hat), water, and proper shoes. (Locals roll their eyes at the many tourists who wear flip-flops on the trails.)

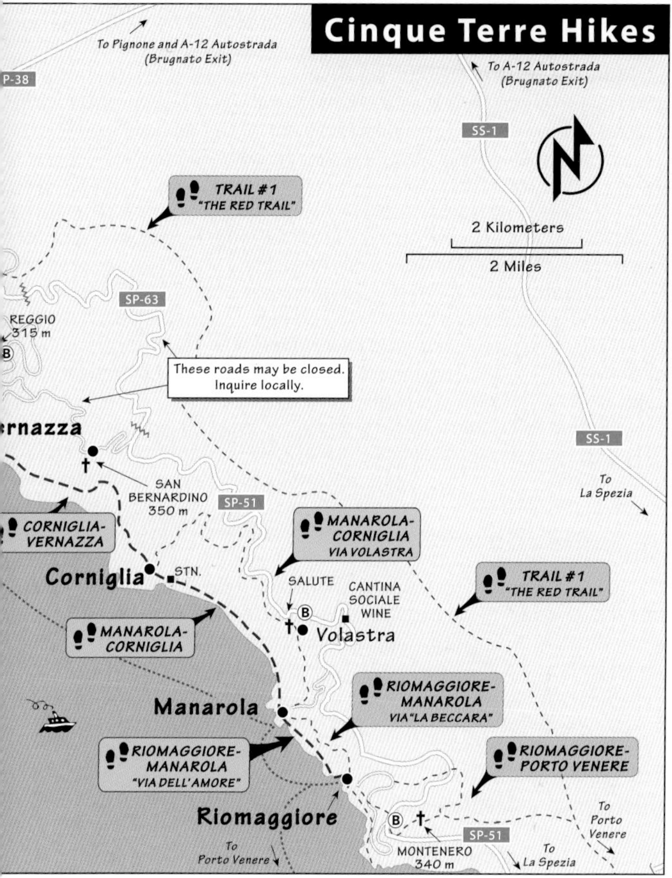

Bug spray can also be useful. And keep in mind that going down can be more challenging (vertigo, shaky knees) than going up. Pace yourself. While the main coastal trail is strenuous, it's doable for any fit hiker...and worth the sweat.

Before embarking on the more difficult hikes, get advice from a national park office (located at each train station), or from Christine and Nicola at Cinque Terre Trekking in Manarola (see page 103).

Shuttle Buses: The ATC shuttle buses (see page 22) can make the going easier, connecting coastal villages to trailheads higher up. Wherever shuttles will save steps, I've mentioned them in the hike description.

When to Go: The coastal trail can be extremely crowded and very hot at midday. For the best light, coolest temperatures, and fewest crowds, start your hike early (say, by 8:00) or late (by 16:00). Before setting out for an evening hike, find out when the sun will set, and leave yourself plenty of time to arrive at your destination before then; there's no lighting on the trails.

Navigation: Maps aren't necessary for the basic coastal hikes. But for the more challenging routes that leave the crowds behind, pick up a good hiking map (about €5, sold everywhere). The national park recently renumbered its trails (using three digits), but many locals still think in terms of the old trail numbers (one digit). I've listed both.

Guided Hikes and Excursions: Your park ticket includes guided hikes and other local excursions (such as town walking tours), which take place several times each month. Even without a valid park ticket, these events are still cheap to attend—usually around €2.50. Look for schedules locally, or email visiteguidate@ati5terre.it for details. (These are also listed at www.visitvernazza.org.)

Give a Hoot: To leave the park cleaner than you found it, bring a plastic bag *(sacchetto di plastica)* on your hike and pick up a little trail trash along the way. It would be great if American visitors—who get so much joy out of this region—were known for this good deed. Note that while the trails themselves are part of the national park, the property to either side is private (no nibbling on veggies or grapes from the vines).

The Main Coastal Trail (Riomaggiore-Monterosso)

The seven-mile coastal trail (officially trail "SVA," a.k.a. "the Blue Trail" or #592) is the ultimate Cinque Terre experience. Unfortunately, big chunks of it are often closed. The trail between Riomaggiore and Manarola—the famed Via dell'Amore—has been closed off and on for years, but hopes are high that soon it will reopen permanently. However, the stretch between Manarola and Corniglia sits under unstable slopes, and is likely to be closed indefinitely.

The sections of the main coastal trail most likely to be open during your visit are also the most challenging and crowded: Corniglia to Vernazza, and Vernazza to Monterosso. Check locally for updates, as trail conditions often change. Remember that hikers need to pay a fee to use the main coastal trail (see "Cinque Terre Park Cards," earlier).

If all sections are open, the entire seven-mile coastal hike can be done by fit hikers in about four hours, but allow five or six for dawdling. Germans (with their task-oriented *Alpenstock* walking sticks) are notorious for rushing too fast through the region. Take it slow...smell the cactus flowers and herbs, notice the scurrying lizards, listen to birds singing in the olive groves, and enjoy vistas on all sides.

If sections of the coastal trail are closed, you can fill in the gaps by train or, far more scenically, by boat. Or choose an alternative hiking route: I've listed these for Riomaggiore to Manarola, and from Manarola to Corniglia.

▲▲▲Riomaggiore-Manarola Hike
(20 minutes; may be closed)

The easiest stretch, the popular Via dell'Amore, was washed out by a landslide in 2012; it may reopen soon. If it's open: In Riomaggiore, facing the train station, go up the stairs to the right, following signs for *Via dell'Amore.*

The Via dell'Amore is the easiest stretch (but may be closed).

The photo-worthy promenade—wide enough for baby strollers—winds along the coast to Manarola. While there's no beach along the trail, stairs lead down to sunbathing rocks. A long tunnel and mega-nets protect hikers from mean-spirited falling rocks. A recommended wine bar—Bar & Vini A Piè de Mà—is located at the Riomaggiore trailhead and offers light meals, awesome town views, and clever boat storage under the train tracks. There's a picnic zone with a water fountain, shade, and a seagull that must have been human in a previous life hanging out just above the Manarola station (WC at Manarola station).

Alternative Route—▲Riomaggiore-Manarola Hike via "La Beccara" *(1.5 hours)*

Trail #531 goes up and over the mountain between these two towns. But be warned: It's essentially stairs all the way up, then all the way down—"shorter," but more intense and dizzying than other parts of the coastal trail. Fit hikers with proper footwear can handle it.

▲Manarola-Corniglia Hike *(45 minutes; likely closed)*

The walk from Manarola to Corniglia is likely closed indefinitely. When open, it's a little longer, more rugged, and steeper than the Via dell'Amore—and also less romantic. To avoid the last stretch of switchback stairs leading up to hill-capping Corniglia, end your hike at its lower-level train station and catch the shuttle bus up to Corniglia's town center (2/hour).

Alternative Route—▲▲Manarola-Corniglia Hike via Volastra *(2.5 hours)*

This challenging hike from Manarola leads up to the village of Volastra, then north through high-altitude vineyard terraces, and steeply down through a forest to Corniglia (about four miles total). You can shave the two steepest miles off this route by taking the shuttle bus from Manarola up to Volastra (about hourly, 15-minute trip).

If you'd rather hike to Volastra, you have two options: The national park's official route (trail #6/#506) cuts up through the valley. But locals have cleared a more scenic alternate route that begins with the vineyard hike on my self-guided walk for Manarola (page 97); partway along this walk, where you reach the wooden religious scenes scampering up the hillside, take a sharp right and walk uphill, following signs for *Panoramico*

The high trail to Volastra offers breathtaking views.

Volastra (Corniglia). While steeper than the official route, this trail follows the ridge at the top of the vineyard, with wonderful sea views.

Tiny **Volastra,** perched between Manarola and Corniglia, hosts lots of Germans and Italians in the summer. Just below town, in the hamlet of Groppo, is Cantina Sociale, a cooperative winery open to the public (wine tastings, www.cantinacinqueterre.com). When you're ready to head for Corniglia, make your way to the village church (where the shuttle bus drops off) and look for *Corniglia* signs. From the front door of the church, directly across the piazza, find the trailhead (marked by an iron cross) for trail #6d/#586 to Case Pianca.

Here begins one of the region's finest hikes, tight-roping along narrow trails tucked between vineyard terraces, with spectacular bird's-eye views over the entire Cinque Terre. You'll cut up and down the terraces a bit—just keep following the red-and-white markings and arrows. After passing a little village (and following signs through someone's seaview backyard), the trail enters a forest and begins its sharp, rocky descent into Corniglia. (To skip the descent, backtrack to Volastra and return by shuttle bus to

Manarola.) High above Corniglia, you'll reach a fork, where you turn left to proceed downhill on trail #7a/#587 to Corniglia.

▲▲▲Corniglia-Vernazza Hike *(1.5 hours)*

The hike from Corniglia to Vernazza—the wildest and greenest section of the coast—is very rewarding but very hilly (going the other direction, from Vernazza to Corniglia, is steeper). From the Corniglia train station and beach, zigzag up to the town (via the steep stairs, the longer road, or the shuttle bus). Keep going through vineyards toward Vernazza. After about 10 minutes, you'll see a faded sign to Guvano beach, far beneath you (a nude beach—now essentially closed). The scenic trail continues through lots of fragrant and flowery vegetation into Vernazza. If you need a break before reaching Vernazza, stop at Bar la Torre, with a strip of amazingly scenic and delightfully shady tables perched high above the town.

▲▲Vernazza-Monterosso Hike *(1.5 hours)*

The trail from Vernazza to Monterosso is a scenic up-and-down-a-lot trek and the most challenging of the bunch. (Start in Monterosso if you want to tackle the toughest section, with many steep stairs, while you're fresh.) Trails are narrow, steep, and crumbly in spots, with a lot of steps but easy to follow. The views just out of Vernazza, looking back at the town, are spectacular. From there you'll gradually ascend to 550 feet, passing some scenic waterfalls populated by croaking frogs. You'll find a few scenically positioned picnic tables located about midway along the trail. As you approach Monterosso, you'll descend steeply through vineyards—on very deep, knee-testing stairs—and eventually follow a rivulet to the sea. The last stretch into Monterosso is along a pleasant, paved pathway clinging to the cliff. You'll pop out right at Monterosso's refreshing old town beach.

Extending the Coastal Trail

Beyond the main coastal trail, the national park maintains a free, extensive network of trails. The Cinque Terre Park Card is not required for the following hikes.

The most challenging hikes—between Riomaggiore and Porto Venere, and especially the High Route linking Porto Venere and Levanto—are best for experienced, fit hikers who can navigate on their own and have

A level promenade links Levanto to Bonassola.

hiking boots, poles, a phone for emergencies, plenty of water, and a good map. Before attempting either hike, get detailed local advice.

To the North

▲Monterosso-Levanto Hike
(3 hours)

This strenuous, rugged-and-wild hike on the coastal trail (SVA) will take you all the way into Levanto. Wear good shoes and be sure to bring lots of water.

Starting from Monterosso, look for signs for the coastal trail at the west end of the new town, and head steeply up. You'll hike up and over Punta Mesco, the bluff that separates the two towns. The first stretch, out of Monterosso, is almost entirely big steps; the rest is mostly a gradual up-and-down.

For a short scenic detour, look for trail #1/#591 not far out of Monterosso. This brief jog leads to the ruined chapel of Sant'Antonio.

To begin the hike in Levanto, see page 129.

Alternative Routes—Monterosso-Levanto Hike via Colle di Gritta
You can enjoy a **higher hike** by skipping the steepest stretch and riding one of Monterosso's shuttle buses to Colle di Gritta (at Hotel Monterosso Alto). From there, follow trail #1/#591 along the ridge and down to Colle di Bagari, where several trails intersect. You can follow trail #571c from here or go a little lower to #571—both head down to trail SVA and Levanto. Or, to make your **hike a loop** that returns directly to Monterosso, continue from Colle di Bagari along trail #1/#591 to trail SVA, and drop steeply into Monterosso.

▲Levanto-Bonassola Hike
(30 minutes)
For an easy excursion, take the train to Levanto, then stroll (or better yet, bike) the level, rails-to-trails promenade to the beach town of Bonassola (see page 130). This is an especially good plan for skipping out on the Cinque Terre crowds.

To the South

▲Riomaggiore-Porto Venere Hike
(5 hours)
For this challenging trek, you'll hike up from Riomaggiore on trail #3/#593 (a continuation of the coastal trail SVA) to the sanctuary at Montenero, then up to Colle del Telegrafo; and then all the way down to Porto Venere on trail #1/AV5T. Partway along, the town of Campiglia has a little bar/restaurant (and buses to La Spezia).

High Route Between Porto Venere and Levanto

Trail #1
Above the coastal trails, and higher than the sanctuary trails, is the demanding 22-mile trail #1 (or #591) connecting Porto Venere to Levanto—and offering sky-high views over the Cinque Terre seafront. Also called "the Red Trail" and marked on maps as "AV5T"—*alta via* ("high route") *5 Terre*—it's cool, uncrowded, and at the top of the world. You could do all or part of this trail.

You can hike to sanctuaries and cemeteries above the towns.

Other Cinque Terre Walks and Hikes

For each Cinque Terre town, I include a **self-guided walk** to help you explore the town (anytime, day or night). Manarola's is the most scenic, offering an easy, rewarding stroll through vineyards with stunning views. Per town, I also list a few easy hiking options, even as simple as walking just outside of town to get a lovely overview looking back (e.g., for Vernazza and Manarola).

Sanctuary Trails (La Strada dei Santuari)

Each of the five towns has its own sanctuary (with a chapel or church dedicated to the Virgin Mary), hovering in the hills a mile or two above town, and accessible by a long, steep hike—quiet and uncrowded.

Villagers feel deeply connected to these spiritual retreats, where they remember lost relatives and feel part of a timeless community. A network of "sanctuary trails" (no hiking card required) crisscrosses the hills above the main coastal route. There's no single path, but with a good map you can link up these moderately difficult trails. In most towns, the shuttle bus can take you from the town center to the sanctuary—you could ride up and hike down. The Cinque Terre Park Card is not required for the hikes.

My favorite is the sanctuary hike from **Vernazza to Reggio** (see page 72). A longer hike connects the sanctuaries of **Monterosso** and **Vernazza** (see page 48). The sanctuary hike from **Riomaggiore to Montenero** is also worth considering (page 117).

Monterosso al Mare

This is a resort with a few cars and lots of hotels, rentable beach umbrellas, crowds, and a little more late-night action than the neighboring towns. Monterosso al Mare—the only Cinque Terre town with some flat land—has two parts: A new town (called Fegina) with a parking lot, train station, and TI; and an old town (Centro Storico), which cradles Old World charm in its small, crooked lanes. In the old town, you'll find hole-in-the-wall shops, rustic pastel townscapes, and a new generation of creative small-businesspeople eager to keep their visitors happy. A handy pedestrian tunnel connects the old with the new.

Strolling the waterfront promenade, you can pick out each of the Cinque Terre towns decorating the coast. After dark, they sparkle. Monterosso is the most enjoyable of the five for backpackers (or the young-at-heart) wanting to connect with others looking for a little nightlife.

ORIENTATION TO MONTEROSSO

Tourist Information

The TI Proloco is next to the train station (mid-April-mid-Oct daily 9:00-18:30, shorter hours off-season, baggage storage, exit station and go left a few doors, tel. 0187-817-506, www.prolocomonterosso.it). For national park cards and information, head upstairs within the station to the ticket office near platform 1 (usually daily 8:00-20:00, shorter hours off-season).

Arrival in Monterosso

By Train: Train travelers arrive in the new town. To reach most of my recommended hotels in the new town, turn right from the station (as you face the water). To get to the old town, turn left from the station, follow the seafront promenade, then duck through the tunnel just before the point—it's a scenic, flat 10-minute stroll.

Notice the bar at track 1, which overlooks both the tracks and the beach. This is a handy place (serving salads, sandwiches, drinks) to hang out while waiting for a train to pull in. As many trains run late, this can turn a frustration into a blessing.

ATC **shuttle buses** run along the waterfront between the old town (Piazza Garibaldi, just beyond the tunnel), the train station, and the parking lot at the end of Via Fegina (*Campo Sportivo* stop). The bus saves you a 10-minute schlep with your bags but only goes once an hour. A few of these shuttles go farther into the hills, making hikes easier by sparing you the initial climb.

Taxis usually wait outside the train station, but if not, you may have to call (€7 from station to old town, mobile 335-616-5842, 335-616-5845, or 335-628-0933).

By Car: Monterosso is 30 minutes off the freeway (exit: Carrodano-Levanto). Note that about three miles above Monterosso, there's an intersection where you must choose either *Monterosso Centro Storico* (old part of town with the Loreto garage) or *Monterosso Fegina* (new town and

Walk Monterosso's beach promenade or head uphill for an overview.

beachfront parking). Know where you want to go, because you can't drive directly between the new town and old center (the tunnel is closed to cars without special permits).

Most drivers should choose the *Fegina* fork. Parking is easy (except July-Aug and weekends in June) in the new town in the huge beachfront guarded lot (€18/24 hours). If instead you head to the old town, you'll find the Loreto parking garage on Via Roma, a 10-minute downhill walk to the main square (€1.70/hour, €18/24 hours).

Helpful Hints

Medical Help: The town's bike-riding, leather bag-toting, English-speaking physician is **Dr. Vitone** (simple visit-€50-100, less for poor students, mobile 338-853-0949, vitonee@yahoo.it).

Thursday Morning Market: Every Thursday morning (8:00-13:00), trucks pull into the old town and fill the public area by the beach with stalls selling produce and more.

Baggage Storage: The **TI** next to the station will store bags (€6/day—but confirm closing time). **Wash and Dry Lavarapido,** two blocks from the station, provides a €5 bag-check service (see next).

Laundry: For full-service, same-day laundry in the new town, try **Wash and Dry Lavarapido.** They'll pick up at your hotel, or you can drop it at their shop. The owners speak little English, so ask your hotelier to arrange the details (€13/load, daily 8:00-19:00, Via Molinelli 17, mobile 339-484-0940, Lucia and Ivano). In the old town, head to **Luètu Lavanderia,** uphill on Via Roma and across from the post office (€4/wash, daily 8:00-20:00, maybe later in summer, tel. 328-286-1908).

Massage: Giorgio Moggia, a physiotherapist, gives good massages at your hotel or in his studio (€70/hour, mobile 339-314-6127, giomogg@tin.it).

MONTEROSSO WALK

This self-guided walk will introduce you to Monterosso, beginning in the old town with an easy and lazy sweep of the sights as seen from the breakwater. Part 1, focusing on the mostly level town center, takes about 30 minutes; for Part 2, summiting the adjacent hill, allow another hour or so.

Part 1: Monterosso Harbor and Town Center

► *Hike out from the dock in the old town and stand along the edge of the concrete breakwater. (If you're visiting by boat, you'll arrive here.)*

Breakwater

From this point you can survey Monterosso's old town (straight ahead) and new town (stretching to the left, with train station and parking lot). Notice the bluff that separates old and new, and imagine how much harder your commute would be if the narrow road tethering these two towns were somehow cut off. It happened in the spring of 2013, when the wall below the hill-topping Capuchin church gave way in a landslide. For a time, the only way to connect the two halves of town by car was to drive six miles around; on foot, you had to hike up and over this hill.

Looking to the right, you can actually see all *cinque* of the *terre* from one spot: Vernazza, Corniglia (above the shore), Manarola, and a few buildings of Riomaggiore beyond that.

These days, the harbor hosts more paddleboats than fishing boats. Sand erosion is a major problem. The partial breakwater (a row of giant rocks in the middle of the harbor) is designed to save the beach from washing away. While old-timers remember a vast beach, their grandchildren truck in sand each spring to give tourists something to bask on. (The Nazis liked the Cinque Terre, too—find two of their bomb-hardened bunkers, near left and far right.)

The fancy four-star Hotel Porto Roca (the pink building high on the hill, on the far right of the harbor) marks the trail to Vernazza. High above,

Monterosso's old town and church are tucked beyond the tracks.

you see an example of the costly roads built in the 1980s to connect the Cinque Terre towns with the freeway over the hills.

The two prominent capes (Punta di Montenero to the right, and Punta Mesco to the left) define the Cinque Terre region. The closer Punta Mesco is part of a protected marine sanctuary and home to a rare seagrass that provides an ideal home for fish eggs. Buoys keep fishing boats away. The cape was once a quarry, providing employment to locals who chipped out the stones used to build the local towns (the greenish stones making up part of the breakwater are from there).

On the far end of the new town, marking the best free beach around, you can just see the statue named *Il Gigante* (hard to spot because it blends in with the gray rock). It's 45 feet tall and once held a trident. While it looks as if it were hewn from the rocky cliff, it's actually made of reinforced concrete and dates from the beginning of the 20th century, when it supported a dancing terrace for a *fin de siècle* villa. A violent storm left the giant holding nothing but memories of Monterosso's glamorous age.

▶ *From the breakwater, walk toward the old town and under the train tracks. Then venture right into the square and find the statue of a dandy holding what looks like a box cutter (near the big playground).*

Piazza Garibaldi

The statue honors Giuseppe Garibaldi, the dashing firebrand revolutionary who, in the 1860s, helped unite the people of Italy into a modern nation. Facing Garibaldi, with your back to the sea, you'll see (from right to left) the orange city hall (with the European Union flag beside the Italian one) and a big home and recreation center for poor and homeless elderly. You'll also

Monterosso al Mare

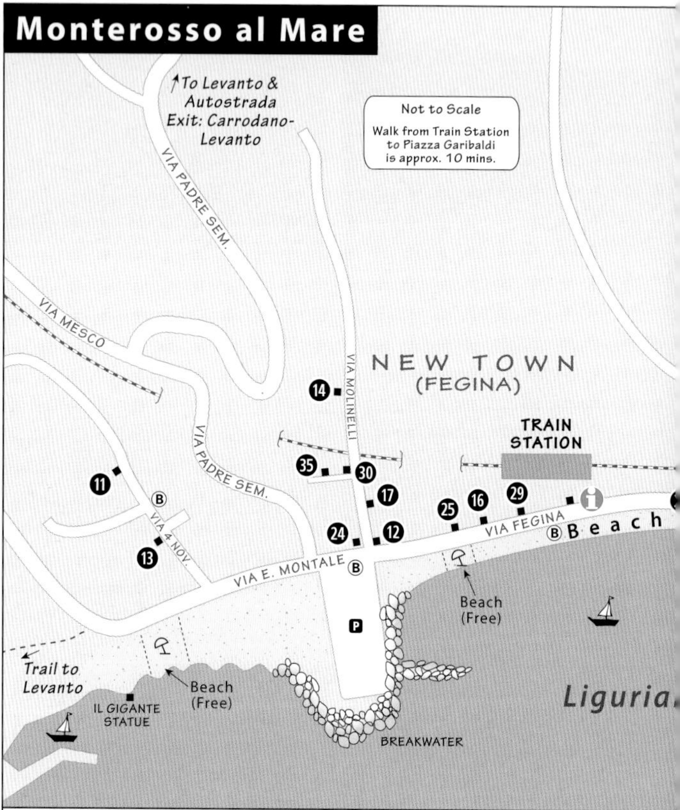

1 Hotel Villa Steno
2 Il Giardino Incantato
3 Albergo Pasquale
4 Locanda il Maestrale
5 Hotel la Colonnina
6 Albergo Marina
7 Buranco Agriturismo
8 Manuel's Guesthouse
9 L'Antica Terrazza & Gastronomia "San Martino"
10 Albergo al Carugio
11 Hotel Villa Adriana
12 Hotel la Spiaggia
13 A Cà du Gigante
14 Hotel Punta Mesco
15 Pensione Agavi
16 Affittacamere Rist. Gabbiano
17 Le Sirene/Raggi di Sole

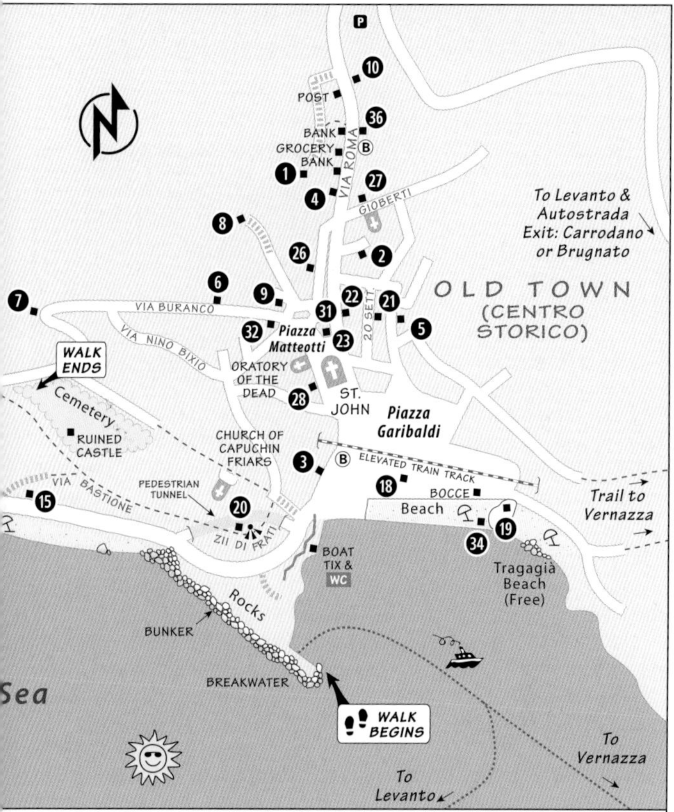

Ristorante Belvedere
Il Casello
Ristorante Tortuga
Via Venti Restaurant
Ristorante al Pozzo
Ciak Restaurant
Miky Restaurant

25 La Cantina di Miky
26 Pizzeria la Smorfia
27 Il Frantoio Focacceria
28 Emy's Way Pizzeria Friggitoria
29 Il Massimo della Focaccia

30 La Bottega SMA
31 Fast Bar
32 Enoteca da Eliseo
33 Nuovo Eden Bar
34 Beach Bar Alga
35 Laundry & Bag Check
36 Launderette

The Cinque Terre Flood and Recovery

On October 25, 2011, after a dry summer, a heavy rainstorm hit the Cinque Terre. Within four hours, 22 inches of rain fell. Flash floods rushed down the hillsides, picking up mud, rocks, trees, furniture, and even cars and buses in their raging, destructive path through the streets down to the sea. Part of Monterosso's old town and Vernazza's main drag were buried under a dozen feet of mud. Four villagers from Vernazza lost their lives.

Today, you'll find the Cinque Terre is back to normal. Most visitors wouldn't even notice that in the affected areas of Monterosso and Vernazza, everything is new: stoves, tables, chairs, and plates. Strolling through these towns today, appreciate the resilience of the human spirit.

see A Ca' du Sciensa restaurant, which has historic town photos inside and upstairs; you're welcome to pop in for a look.

Just under the bell tower (with your back to the sea, it's on your left), a set of covered arcades facing the sea is where the old-timers hang out (they see all and know all). The crenellated bell tower marks the church.

▶ *Go to church.*

Church of St. John the Baptist (Chiesa di San Giovanni Battista)

First, walk alongside the church, past the arcade. Near the second side door, find the high-water mark *(altezza massima)* from an October 1966 flood—which also famously devastated Florence. Nearby, a second (higher) plaque commemorates the 2011 flood.

Now hook left, around the church—which is where you'll find its black-and-white-striped main facade. With white marble from Carrara and green marble from Punta Mesco, the church is typical of the region's Romanesque style. Note the lacy, stone rose window above the entrance. It's as delicate as crochet work, with 18 slender mullions (the petals of the rose). The marble stripes get narrower the higher they go, creating the illusion that the church is taller than it really is.

Step inside for more Ligurian Gothic: original marble columns and capitals with pointed arches to match. The octagonal baptismal font (in the back of the church) was carved from Carrara marble in 1359. Imagine the job getting that from the quarries, about 40 miles away. In the chapel to the right of the high altar, look for the wooden statue of St. Anthony, carved about 1400, which once graced a church that stood atop Punta Mesco. The church itself dates from 1307—see the proud inscription on the left-middle column: "MilloCCCVII."

▶ *Leaving the church, immediately turn left and go to church again.*

Oratory of the Dead (Oratorio dei Neri): During the Counter-Reformation, the Catholic Church offset the rising influence of the Lutherans by creating brotherhoods of good works. These religious Rotary clubs were called "confraternities." Monterosso had two, nicknamed White and Black. This building is the oratory of the Black group, whose mission—as the macabre decor filling the interior indicates—was to arrange for funerals and take care of widows, orphans, the shipwrecked, and the souls of those who ignore the request for a €1 donation. It dates from the 16th century, and membership has passed from father to son for generations. Notice the fine, carved choir stalls (c. 1700), just inside the door, and the haunted-house chandeliers. Look up at the ceiling to find the symbol of the confraternity: a skull-and-crossbones and an hourglass...death awaits us all.

▶ *On that cheery note, if you're in a lazy mood, you can discreetly split off from our walking tour now to enjoy strolling, shopping, gelato-licking, a day at the beach...or all of the above. But if you're up for a hike, continue with me on Part 2. As you face out to sea, look to the right and imagine the view from the top of that hill. Now...go see it.*

Part 2: Capuchin Church and Hilltop Cemetery

▶ *Return to the beach and find the brick steps that lead up to the hill-capping church (between the train tracks and the pedestrian tunnel, and passing in front of Albergo Pasquale). Approaching the bend in the path, watch for the stairs leading steeply and sharply to the right. This lane (Salita dei Cappuccini) is nicknamed Zii di Frati, or...*

Switchbacks of the Friars

Follow the yellow brick road (OK, it's orange...but I couldn't help singing

St. Francis graces a Ligurian Sea viewpoint.

as I skipped skyward). Pause at the terrace above the seaside castle at a statue of St. Francis and a wolf taking in a grand view. Enjoy another opportunity to see all five of the Cinque Terre towns. From here, backtrack 20 yards and continue uphill.

▸ *When you reach a gate marked Convento e Chiesa Cappuccini, you have arrived at the...*

Church of the Capuchin Friars

The former monastery is now manned by a single caretaker friar. Before stepping inside, notice the church's striped Romanesque facade. It's all fake. Tap it—no marble, just cheap 18th-century stucco. Go inside and sit in the rear pew. The high altarpiece painting of St. Francis can be rolled up on special days to reveal a statue of Mary standing behind it. Look at the statue of St. Anthony to the right and smile (you're on convent camera). Wave at the security camera—they're nervous about the precious painting to your left.

This fine painting of the **Crucifixion** is attributed to Anthony van Dyck, the 17th-century Flemish master who lived and worked for years in nearby Genoa (though art historians suspect that, at best, it was painted by someone in the artist's workshop). When Jesus died, the earth went dark. Notice the eclipsed sun in the painting, just to the right of the cross. Do the electric candles work? Pick one up, pray for peace, and plug it in. (Leave €0.50, or unplug it and put it back.)

▸ *Leave and turn left through another gate to hike 100 yards uphill to the cemetery filling the ruined castle at the top of the hill. Reaching the cemetery's gate, look back and enjoy the view over the town.*

Cemetery in the Ruined Castle

In the Dark Ages, the village huddled within this castle. Slowly it expanded. Notice the town view from here—no sea. You're looking at the oldest part of Monterosso, tucked behind the hill, out of view of 13th-century pirates.

Respectfully explore the cemetery. Ponder the black-and-white photos of grandparents past. Read the headstones: *Q.R.P.* is *Qui Riposa in Pace* (a.k.a. R.I.P.). Rich families had their own little tomb buildings. That this is still a place treasured by the living is demonstrated by the abundance of fresh flowers.

Climb to the very summit—the castle's keep, or place of last refuge. Priests are buried in a line of graves closest to the sea, but facing inland, toward the town's holy sanctuary high on the hillside (above the road, with its triangular steeple peeking above the trees). Each Cinque Terre town has a lofty sanctuary, dedicated to Mary and dear to the village hearts.

▸ *Your tour is over—any trail leads you back into town.*

EXPERIENCES IN MONTEROSSO

Hikes from Monterosso

For a relatively easy in-town hike, "Part 2" of my self-guided Monterosso Walk (above) takes you on a rewarding climb up to the **hilltop cemetery** in the middle of town.

Several ambitious hikes begin in Monterosso; you can use **shuttle buses** (see "Arrival in Monterosso") to make challenging hikes easier.

If you're hiking to **Vernazza** on the main coastal trail, you can skip the many steep stairs at the start of the trail by riding the bus to Vettora. If heading north over the Punta Mesco bluff to **Levanto,** you can ride up

The sandy new town beach is busier than the gravel old town beach.

to Colle di Gritta—which makes most of the rest of the hike downhill. (For more on these hikes, see page 23.)

You can hike to Monterosso's **Soviore sanctuary** (on trail #9/#509) or take the shuttle bus. To hike from Soviore to Vernazza's **Reggio sanctuary,** follow a mostly level trail (#1/#591) to Termine, then head down to Reggio (on #8b/#582), then very steeply downhill into Vernazza (on #8/#508). Allow 2.5 hours, if you start with the shuttle bus.

Locals know all the options—and shuttle bus schedules—so ask around. But be aware that only one or two buses a day, and only in summer, head into the high country.

Beaches

Monterosso's **new town** has easily the Cinque Terre's best—and most crowded—beach (immediately in front of the train station). Most of the beach is technically private, where you'll pay €20-25 to rent two chairs and an umbrella for the day (a worthwhile investment if you're lingering; prices get very soft in the afternoon). Light lunches are served by beach cafés to sunbathers at their lounge chairs. Various outfits along here rent kayaks and stand-up paddleboards (look for signs at the west end of the beach—near the parking lot—or ask around). If there are no umbrellas on a stretch of beach, it's public, so you can spread out a towel anywhere. There's a free beach at the far-west end, near the Gigante statue; others are marked on the map on page 42.

The **old town** also has its own, predominantly private beach; rent umbrellas, chairs, kayaks, and paddleboats from Beach Bar Alga, which is also a scenic spot for a drink. Tucked just beyond the private beach—under the Il Casello restaurant at the east end of town—is the free public beach called Tragagià, which is gravelly and generally less crowded. The bocce ball court (next to Il Casello) is busy with older men enjoying their favorite pastime.

Wine Tasting

Buranco Agriturismo offers visits to their vineyard and cantina, if you reserve at least two days in advance. You'll taste some of their wines plus a *grappa* (firewater) and a *limoncino,* along with home-cooked food (€20-30/person with snacks, English may be limited, follow Via Buranco uphill to path, 10 minutes above town, also rents recommended apartments, tel. 0187-817-677, www.burancocinqueterre.it).

Boat Rides

In addition to the regularly scheduled big boats (see page 18), you can hire your own captain for transfers to other towns or for a longer cruise. For example, **Stefano** has two six-person boats: the *Matilde* and the *Babaah* (about €100/hour, one hour is enough for a quick spin, two hours includes time for swimming stops; longer trips to Porto Venere and offshore islands possible; mobile 333-821-2007, www.matildenavigazione.com, info@matildenavigazione.com).

NIGHTLIFE IN MONTEROSSO

Although I've listed these establishments for their nightlife, they work any time of day for a drink and spot to relax, especially the beach bars.

Enoteca da Eliseo, my favorite wine bar in town, comes with operatic ambience. Eliseo and his wife, Mary, love music and wine. Taste by the glass *(bicchiere),* or select a fine bottle from their shop shelf and enjoy it and the village action from their cozy tables. Eliseo stocks more than a hundred varieties of grappa (Wed-Mon 14:00-23:30, closed Tue, Piazza Matteotti 3, a block inland behind church, tel. 0187-817-308).

Fast Bar, the best bar in town for young travelers and night owls, is located on Via Roma in the old town. Customers mix travel tales with big, cold beers, and the crowd (and the rock 'n' roll) gets noisier as the night rolls on. Come here to watch Italian or American sporting events on TV all day (cheap *panini,* salads, and other light meals usually served until

Monterosso's beachfront is beautiful on a balmy evening.

midnight, open Fri-Wed 9:30-late, closed Thu except in peak season; Alex, Francesco, and Stefano).

La Cantina di Miky, in the new town just beyond the train station, is a trendy bar-restaurant with an extensive cocktail and *grappa* menu; they sometimes host live music. The seating is in three zones: overlooking the beach, in the garden, or in the cellar. Try the fun "five villages" wine tasting with local meats and cheeses (€15/person for just wine, €20/person with food). This is the best place in town for top-end Italian microbrews (Thu-Tue until late, closed Wed, Via Fegina 90, tel. 0187-802-525).

Beach Bars: On a balmy evening, enjoy a memorable drink with a view of swimmers, sunbathers, and the languid Ligurian Sea. In the new town, try **Nuovo Eden Bar,** overlooking the beach by the big rock (€6 cocktails, drinks come with a light snack, good ice cream, open long hours daily but closed Mon off-season). In the old town, **Beach Bar Alga** has an island ambience (daily until 20:00).

SLEEPING IN MONTEROSSO

Monterosso, the most beach-resorty of the five Cinque Terre towns, offers maximum comfort and ease. The TI Proloco just outside the train station can give you a list of rooms for rent. Rooms in Monterosso are a better value than similar rooms in crowded Vernazza, and the proprietors seem more genuine and welcoming.

In the Old Town

$$$$ Hotel Villa Steno is lovingly managed and features great view balconies, panoramic gardens and a roof terrace with sun beds, air-conditioning, and the friendly help of Matteo and his wife, Carla. Of their 16 rooms, 14 have view balconies (RS%, family rooms, hearty buffet breakfast, elevator, laundry service, ask about pay parking when you reserve, hike up to their panoramic terrace, Via Roma 109, tel. 0187-817-028 or 0187-818-336, www.villasteno.com, steno@pasini.com). It's a 15-minute climb (or €8 taxi ride) from the train station to the top of the old town. Readers get a free Cinque Terre info packet and a glass of local wine when they check in—ask for it.

$$$$ Il Giardino Incantato ("The Enchanted Garden") is a charming, comfortable four-room B&B with impressive attention to detail in a tastefully renovated 16th-century Ligurian home in the heart of the old town. It's run by kind and eager-to-please Fausto and Mariapia and their gregarious staff. Sip their homemade *limoncino* upon check-in, and have breakfast under lemon trees in a delightful hidden garden, illuminated with candles in the evening (RS%, air-con, free minibar and tea and coffee service, laundry service, Via Mazzini 18, tel. 0187-818-315, mobile 333-264-9252, www.ilgiardinoincantato.net, giardino_incantato@libero.it).

$$$$ Albergo Pasquale is modern and comfortable with 15 seaview rooms, run by the same family as Hotel Villa Steno (listed earlier). Located right on the harbor, it's just a few steps from the beach, boat dock, and tunnel entrance to the new town. While there is some train noise, the soundtrack is mostly a lullaby of waves. It has an elevator and offers easier access than most (RS%, family room, same welcome drink as Villa Steno, air-con, laundry service, Via Fegina 8, tel. 0187-817-550 or 0187-817-477, www.hotelpasquale.it, pasquale@pasini.com, Felicita and Marco).

$$$ Locanda il Maestrale rents six small, stylish rooms in a sophisticated and peaceful little inn. Although renovated with all the modern comforts, it retains centuries-old character under frescoed ceilings. Its peaceful sun terrace overlooking the old town and Via Roma action is a delight. Guests enjoy free drinks and snacks each afternoon (RS%, air-con, Via Roma 37, tel. 0187-817-013, mobile 338-4530-531, www.locandamaestrale.net, maestrale@monterossonet.com, Stefania).

$$$ Hotel la Colonnina has 21 big rooms (some older, some stylishly up-to-date), generous and meticulously cared-for public spaces, a cozy garden, and an inviting shared seaview terrace with sun beds. It's buried in the town's fragrant and sleepy back streets (family rooms, many rooms with private terraces, cash preferred, air-con, fridges, elevator, a block inland from main square at Via Zuecca 6, tel. 0187-817-439, www.lacolonninacinqueterre.it, info@lacolonninacinqueterre.it, Cristina).

$$$ Albergo Marina, creatively run by enthusiastic husband-and-wife team Marina and Eraldo, has 23 pleasant rooms and a garden with lemon trees. With a free and filling buffet featuring local specialties each afternoon, they offer a fine value (RS%, family rooms, elevator, air-con, free kayak and snorkel equipment, Via Buranco 40, tel. 0187-817-613, www.hotelmarina5terre.com, marina@hotelmarina5terre.com).

$$$ Buranco Agriturismo, a 10-minute hike above the old town, has wonderful gardens and views over the vine-covered valley. Its primary business is wine and olive-oil production (and they host wine tastings), but they also offer three apartments. It's a rare opportunity to stay in a farmhouse but still be able to get to town on foot (air-con, €10 taxi from station, tel. 0187-817-677, mobile 349-434-8046, www.burancocinqueterre.it, info@buranco.it, informally run by Loredana, Mary, and Giulietta).

$$$ Manuel's Guesthouse, perched high above the town among terraces, is a garden getaway run by Lorenzo and his father, Giovanni. They have six big, bright rooms and a grand view. After climbing the killer stairs from the town center, their killer terrace is hard to leave—especially after a few drinks (cash only, air-con, up about 100 steps behind church—you can ask Lorenzo to carry your bags up the hill, Via San Martino 39, mobile 333-439-0809, www.manuelsguesthouse.com, manuelsguesthouse@libero.it).

$$ L'Antica Terrazza rents five classy rooms right in town. With a pretty terrace overlooking the pedestrian street and minimal stairs, Raffaella and John offer a good deal (RS%, cheaper room with private bath down the hall, air-con, Vicolo San Martino 1, mobile 380-138-0082 or 347-132-6213, www.anticaterrazza.com, post@anticaterrazza.com).

$ Albergo al Carugio has nine practical rooms in a big apartment-style building at the top of the old town. It's quiet, comfy, and a fine budget value (RS%, no breakfast, air-con—but only during the daytime June-Sept, Via Roma 100, tel. 0187-817-453, www.alcarugio.it, info@alcarugio.it, conscientiously run by Andrea).

In the New Town

$$$$ Hotel Villa Adriana is big, contemporary, and bright, set on a church-owned estate with a peaceful garden, a pool, free parking, and a no-stress style. They rent 54 rooms—some with terraces and/or sea views—ask for one when you reserve, but no guarantees (family rooms, air-con, elevator, free loaner bikes, affordable dinners, Via IV Novembre 23, tel. 0187-818-109, www.villaadriana.info, info@villaadriana.info).

$$$$ Hotel la Spiaggia, facing the beach, is a venerable old place with 19 rooms—half with sea views (cash only, air-con, elevator, free parking—reserve in advance, Via Lungomare 96, tel. 0187-817-567, www.laspiaggiahotel.com, hotellaspiaggia@libero.it, Maria and her dad, Andrea).

$$$ A Cà du Gigante, despite its name, is a tiny yet chic refuge with nine rooms. About 100 yards from the beach (and surrounded by blocky apartments and big hotels on a modern street), the interior is tastefully done with upscale comfort in mind (RS%, air-con, limited free parking, Via IV Novembre 11, tel. 0187-817-401, www.ilgigantecinqueterre.it, gigante@ilgigantecinqueterre.it, Claudia).

$$$ Hotel Punta Mesco is a tidy, well-run little haven renting 17 quiet, casual rooms at a good price. While none have views, 10 rooms have small terraces (RS%, family room, air-con, parking, Via Molinelli 35, tel. 0187-817-495, www.hotelpuntamesco.it, info@hotelpuntamesco.it, Roberto, Diego, and Manuel).

$$$ Pensione Agavi has 10 spartan, bright, overpriced rooms along the waterfront promenade. I'd skip it—unless you can score one of the rooms with a grand view over the beach (cheaper rooms with shared bath, breakfast extra, cash only, refrigerators, turn left out of station to Fegina 30, tel. 0187-817-171, www.hotelagavi.com, info@hotelagavi.com, Hillary).

$$ Affittacamere Ristorante il Gabbiano, a touristy restaurant right on the beach, rents five basic, dated, but affordable rooms upstairs. Three rooms face the sea, with small balconies; two overlook a little garden at the back. Check in at the Gabbiano restaurant (family rooms, cash only, air-con, Via Fegina 84, tel. 0187-817-578, www.affittacamereristoranteilgabbiano.com, affittacamereilgabbiano@live.it).

$ Le Sirene/Raggi di Sole, with nine simple rooms in two humble buildings, is a decent budget choice in this pricey town. It's run from a hole-in-the-wall reception desk a block from the station, just off the water. I'd request the Le Sirene building, which has smaller bathrooms but no train noise, and is a bit more spacious and airy than Raggi di Sole (RS%, family rooms, fans, Via Molinelli 10, mobile 331-788-1088, www.sirenerooms.com, sirenerooms@gmail.com, Ermanna).

EATING IN MONTEROSSO

With a Sea View

$$ Ristorante Belvedere, big and sprawling, is *the* place for a good-value meal indoors or outdoors on the harborfront. Their huge €48 *anfora belvedere*—mixed seafood stew dumped dramatically at the table from a pottery amphora into your bowl—can easily be split among up to four diners. Their *misto mare* plate (2-person minimum, €15/person), a fishy treat, nearly makes an entire meal. Mussel fans will enjoy the *tagliolini della casa.* It's energetically run by Federico and Roberto (Wed-Mon 12:00-14:30 & 18:00-22:00, closed Tue except Aug, on the harbor in the old town, tel. 0187-817-033).

$$ Il Casello is the only place for a fun meal on a terrace overlooking the old town beach. With outdoor tables on a rocky outcrop, it's a pleasant spot for a salad, pasta, or heartier meal (daily April-Oct 12:00-22:00, closed Nov-March, mobile 333-492-7629, Bacco).

$$$ Ristorante Tortuga is the top option in Monterosso for seaview elegance, with gorgeous outdoor seating high on a bluff and a lovely white-tablecloth-and-candles interior. The food doesn't quite live up to the fuss, and the service is uneven, but the setting is memorable. Drop by to choose and reserve a table for later (Tue-Sun 12:00-15:00 & 18:00-21:30, closed Mon; at the tip of the point between the old and new towns—just outside the tunnel at the new town end, or climb up the ramp in front of the old town's Albergo Pasquale; tel. 0187-800-065, mobile 333-240-7956, Silvia and Giamba).

In the Old Town

$$$ Via Venti is a quiet little trattoria, hidden in an alley deep in the heart of the old town, where Papa Ettore and co-chef Ilaria create imaginative seafood dishes using the day's catch and freshly made pasta. Ilaria's husband Michele serves up delicate and savory gnocchi with crab, tender ravioli stuffed with fresh fish, and pear-and-pecorino pasta. The outdoor tables are on a lane as nondescript as the humdrum interior—but you're here for the food (Fri-Wed 12:00-14:30 & 18:30-22:30, closed Thu, Via XX Settembre 32, tel. 0187-818-347).

$ Gastronomia "San Martino," warmly and passionately run by Moreno, is tiny, humble, and almost without ambience. But this excellent-value place serves surprisingly affordable, quality dishes. Eat (from plastic plates) at one of the few tables—inside or out on a pleasant street—or find a driftwood log for a takeaway seafront feast (Tue-Sun 12:00-15:00 & 18:00-22:00, closed Mon, next to recommended L'Antica Terrazza hotel at Vicolo San Martino 2, mobile 346-109-7338).

$$$ Ristorante al Pozzo is a favorite among locals. It's family-run, with good old-fashioned quality, as Gino (with his long white beard) cooks, and his engaging English-speaking son, Manuel, serves. They have one of the best wine lists in town, serve only homemade pasta, and are known for their raw fish and wonderful seafood *antipasti misti* (Fri-Wed 12:00-15:00 & 18:30-22:30, closed Thu, Via Roma 24, tel. 0187-817-575).

$$$ Ciak, high-energy and tightly packed, is a local institution with reliably good food, higher prices, and (sometimes) a bit of an attitude. It's known for its huge, sizzling terra-cotta crock for two crammed with the day's catch and accompanied by risotto or spaghetti, or served swimming in a soup *(zuppa).* Other popular choices are fish ravioli with shrimp sauce and the seafood *antipasto Lampara.* Stroll a couple of paces past the outdoor tables up Via Roma to see what Signore Ciak (who wears his Popeye cap in the kitchen) has on the stove. Reservations are smart in summer (Thu-Tue 12:00-15:00 & 18:00-22:30, closed Wed, Piazza Don Minzoni 6, tel. 0187-817-014, www.ristoranteciak.net).

In the New Town

Even if you're not sleeping in the new town, consider venturing over for dinner at one of these options; as a bonus, the walk is mostly along a scenic and lively beachfront promenade.

$$$$ Miky is packed with well-dressed locals who know their seafood and want to eat it in a classy environment. For elegantly presented, top-quality food that celebrates local ingredients and traditions, this is my Cinque Terre favorite. It's a proud family operation—Miky (dad), Simonetta (mom), charming Sara (daughter, who greets guests)—and the attentive but easygoing waitstaff all work hard. Try their "pizza pasta," served in a bowl topped with a thin pizza crust, then flambéed at your table. Many of the wines on their fine list are available by the glass if you ask. If I were ever to require a dessert, it would be their mixed sampler plate, *dolce misto*—plenty for two (Wed-Mon 12:00-15:00 & 19:00-23:00, closed Tue, reservations wise in summer, in the new town 100 yards from train station at Via Fegina 104, tel. 0187-817-608, www.ristorantemiky.it).

$$$ La Cantina di Miky, a few doors down (toward the station), serves artfully crafted Ligurian specialties that follow in Miky's family tradition of quality. Run by son Manuel—and Christine from New Jersey—it's more youthful and informal, and the setting is unpretentious (sit downstairs, in the garden, or overlooking the sea). The €20 anchovy tasting plate is an education in the many ways to prepare this local specialty (creative desserts, large selection of Italian microbrews, Thu-Tue 12:00-24:00, closed Wed, Via Fegina 90, tel. 0187-802-525). This place doubles as a cocktail bar in the evenings.

Light Meals, Takeout Food, and Breakfast

In the Old Town: Lots of shops and bakeries sell pizza and focaccia to eat in or take out for an easy picnic on the beach or trail. **$ Pizzeria la Smorfia**—a local favorite—cooks up good pizza; a large one can feed three (Fri-Wed 11:00-24:00, closed Thu, Via Vittorio Emanuele 73, tel. 0187-818-395). At **$ Il Frantoio Focacceria,** Simone makes tasty pizza and focaccia (Fri-Wed 9:00-14:00 & 16:30-20:00, closed Thu, just off Via Roma at Via Gioberti 1). **$ Emy's Way Pizzeria Friggitoria** offers thick-crust pizzas—whole and by the slice—and deep-fried seafood in to-go cones (daily 11:00-20:00, later in summer, along the skinny street next to the church; Emiliano).

In the New Town, near the Station: For a quick bite right at the train station (or on the beach), try **$ Il Massimo della Focaccia** for quiche-like tortes, sandwiches, focaccia pizzas, and desserts. With benches just in front, this is a good bet for a light meal with a sea view (Thu-Tue 9:00-19:00, closed Wed except June-Aug, Via Fegina 50 at the station). **La Bottega**

SMA is a smart minimart with fresh produce, *antipasti,* deli items, and other picnic fare. They'll even make you a sandwich: Select a bread and filling, and pay by the weight (daily 8:00-13:00 & 16:30-19:30—except closed Sun afternoon, shorter hours off-season, near Lavarapido at Vittoria Gianni 21).

Breakfast: Most hotels here include breakfast in the room rate. But if you're looking, **Fast Bar** has an American-style breakfast for €10, or cheaper à la carte (see listing under "Nightlife in Monterosso," earlier).

MONTEROSSO CONNECTIONS

Of the five Cinque Terre towns, Monterosso has the most direct train connections with towns outside the Cinque Terre.

From Monterosso by Train to: Levanto (2-3/hour, 4 minutes), **Sestri Levante** (hourly, 30 minutes, most trains to Genoa stop here), **Santa Margherita Ligure** (at least hourly, 45 minutes), **Genoa** (hourly, 1.5 hours; for destinations in France, you'll change trains here), **Milan** (8/day direct, otherwise hourly with change in Genoa, 3 hours), **Venice** (5/day, 6 hours, change in Milan), **La Spezia** (2-3/hour, 15-30 minutes), **Pisa** (hourly, 1-1.5 hours), **Rome** (hourly, 4.5 hours, change in La Spezia).

Vernazza

With the closest thing to a natural harbor—overseen by a ruined castle, a stout stone church, and a Crayola-colored canyon of fisherfolk homes—Vernazza is the jewel of the Cinque Terre. Only the regular noisy slurping up of the train by the mountain reminds you of the modern world.

The action is at the harbor, where you'll find outdoor eateries ringing a humble piazza, a restaurant hanging on the edge of the castle, and a breakwater with a promenade, corralled by a natural amphitheater of terraced hills. In the summer, the beach becomes a soccer field, with teams fielded by bars and restaurants providing late-night entertainment. A summer opera series adds cultural drama. In the dark, locals fish off the promontory, using glowing bobbers that shine in the waves. In the winter, the population shrinks, as many people return to their more comfortable big-city apartments to spend the money they reaped during the tourist season.

Leisure time is devoted to taking part in the *passeggiata*—strolling lazily together up and down the main street. Sit on a bench and study the passersby doing their *vasche* (laps). Explore the characteristic alleys. Learn—and live—the phrase *"la vita pigra di Vernazza"* (the lazy life of Vernazza).

ORIENTATION TO VERNAZZA

Tourist Information

At the train station, you can get answers to basic questions at the gift shop (daily 8:00-20:00, closed in winter) or the ticket desk/park office (likely daily 8:00-20:00, shorter hours off-season, tel. 0187-812-533). Public WCs are just behind. Locals run their own helpful tourist board/website, called Visit Vernazza (www.visitvernazza.org).

Arrival in Vernazza

By Train: Vernazza's train station is only about three train cars long, but the trains themselves are much longer—so most of the cars come to a stop in a long, dark tunnel. Get out anyway, and walk through the tunnel to the station. From there the main street flows through town right down to the harbor. If you're sleeping here, many locals who rent rooms will meet you at the station and walk you to your place (call first to tell them which train you're on).

By Car: Roads to Vernazza are in terrible shape, and parking is strictly limited. My best advice: Don't drive to Vernazza. If you're coming from the north, park in Levanto. If arriving from the south, park your car in La Spezia. From either town, hop on the train. But if you must drive, get precise advice from your hotelier about which roads are open, how to drive in, and where to park. Yellow lines mark parking spots for residents only.

Helpful Hints

Tuesday Morning Market: Vernazza's skimpy business community is augmented Tuesday mornings (8:00-13:00), when a meager gang of cars and trucks pulls into town for a tailgate market. Eros is often among the vendors; his family has sold flowers here for years (and he's also an amazing opera singer).

Baggage Storage: You can leave your bags at the train-station gift shop (€1/hour, €10/day, daily 8:00-20:00, closed in winter). Friendly Francesco and his staff will happily haul your luggage between the train station and your accommodations (€3/piece).

Laundry: A small self-serve launderette is at the top of town next to the post office (€5/wash, €5/dry, daily 7:00-23:00).

Booking Agency: Cinque Terre Riviera, run by Miriana, books vacation rentals in the Cinque Terre towns and La Spezia, including some exclusive properties (ask about discounts). She also sells tickets for Vernazza's summer opera, and can arrange transportation, cooking classes, and weddings (Via Roma 24, mobile 340-794-7358, www.cinqueterreriviera.com, info@cinqueterreriviera.com).

Massage: Kate Allen offers a relaxing fusion of aromatic/Swedish/holistic massage and reflexology in her studio in the center across from the pharmacy (€60/hour, mobile 333-568-4653, www.vernazzamassage5terre.com).

VERNAZZA WALK

This self-guided walk includes Vernazza's characteristic town squares and ends on its scenic breakwater.

► *From the train station, walk under the tracks and uphill about 30 yards until you reach the sharp bend in the road. You'll see a tiny piazza with benches and big millstones.*

"Millstone Square"

The millstones are a reminder that the town stream (which goes underground here) once powered Vernazza's water mill. (You can still see its tiny "river" if you follow this road up a few steps.) Until the 1950s, the river ran openly through the center of town. Old-timers recall the days before the breakwater, when the river cascaded down and the surf sent waves rolling up Vernazza's main drag. (The name "Vernazza" is actually local dialect for "little Venice"; before the main road covered up the stream, the town had a string of charming bridges, evoking those in Venice.)

Corralling this stream under the modern street, and forcing it to take a hard right turn here, contributed to the damage caused by the 2011 flood. After the flood, Swiss engineers redesigned the drainage system, so any

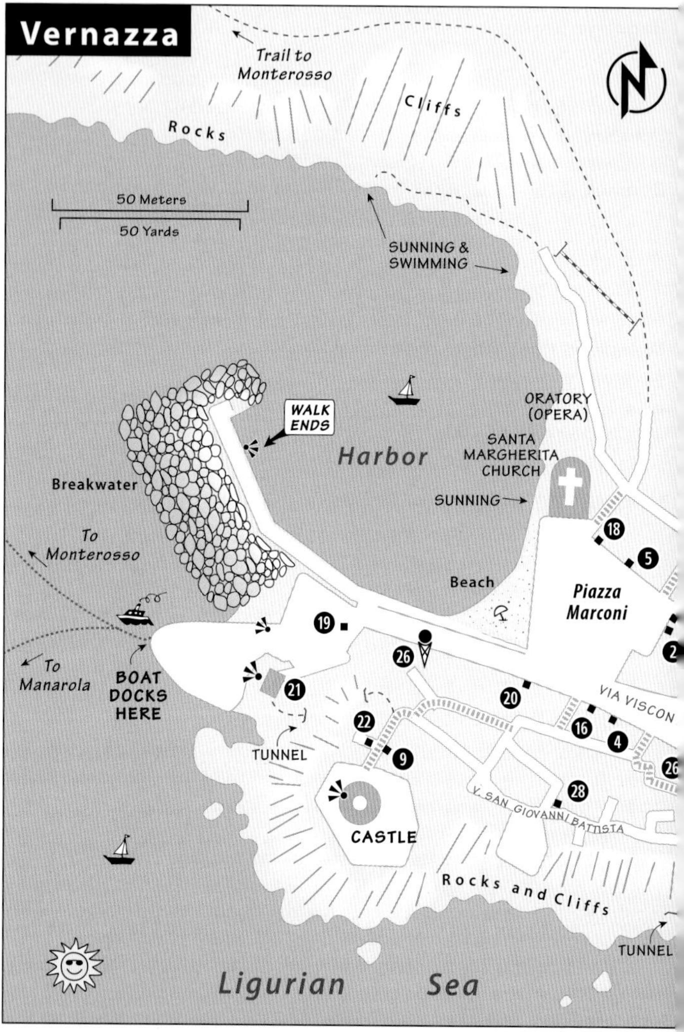
Vernazza
Trail to Monterosso
Cliffs
Rocks
50 Meters
50 Yards
SUNNING & SWIMMING
ORATORY (OPERA)
SANTA MARGHERITA CHURCH
WALK ENDS
Harbor
Breakwater
SUNNING
To Monterosso
Beach
Piazza Marconi
To Manarola
BOAT DOCKS HERE
VIA VISCON
TUNNEL
V. SAN GIOVANNI BATTISTA
CASTLE
Rocks and Cliffs
TUNNEL
Ligurian Sea
18
5
19
26
21
20
16
4
22
9
28

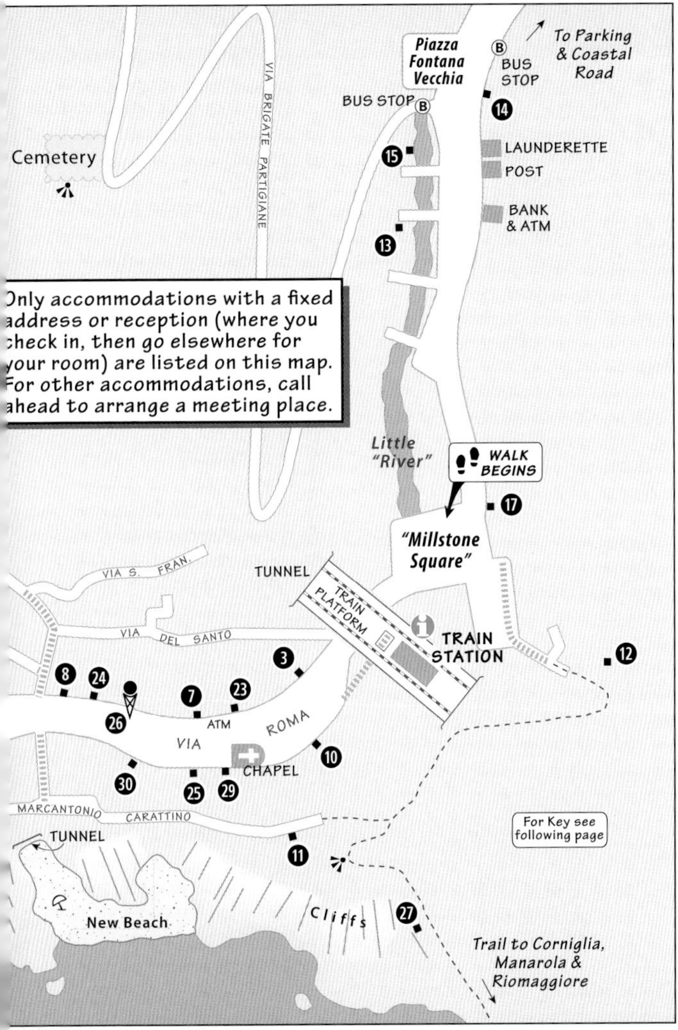
Piazza Fontana Vecchia
BUS STOP
BUS STOP
To Parking & Coastal Road
VIA BRIGATE PARTIGIANE
Cemetery
LAUNDERETTE
POST
BANK & ATM
Only accommodations with a fixed address or reception (where you check in, then go elsewhere for your room) are listed on this map. For other accommodations, call ahead to arrange a meeting place.
Little "River"
WALK BEGINS
"Millstone Square"
TUNNEL
TRAIN PLATFORM
TRAIN STATION
VIA S. FRAN.
VIA DEL SANTO
ATM
VIA ROMA
CHAPEL
MARCANTONIO CARATTINO
TUNNEL
For Key see following page
New Beach
Cliffs
Trail to Corniglia, Manarola & Riomaggiore

Vernazza Hotels & Restaurants

1. La Malà & La Marina Rooms (call first)
2. Francamaria Reception & Albergo Barbara Rooms
3. Vernazza Rooms Reception & Blue Marlin Bar
4. Rosa Vitali Rooms
5. Martina Callo Rooms, Capitano Rooms Reception & Trattoria del Capitano
6. Nicolina Rooms Reception & Ristorante Pizzeria Vulnetia
7. Rooms Francesca Reception (Enoteca Sciacchetrà)
8. Ivo's Camere Reception (Pizzeria Fratelli Basso)
9. Monica Lercari Rooms
10. Eva's Rooms & Trattoria da Sandro
11. Rooms Elisabetta (call first)
12. Giuliano Basso Rooms
13. Camere Fontana Vecchia
14. Tonino Basso Rooms & Il Pirata delle Cinque Terre Café
15. La Rosa dei Venti (call first)
16. Gianni Franzi Reception/Ristorante
17. Pensione Sorriso
18. Ananasso Bar
19. Pizzeria Baia Saracena
20. Gambero Rosso Ristorante
21. Ristorante Belforte
22. Ristorante al Castello
23. Antica Osteria il Baretto
24. Forno Bakery
25. Lunch Box
26. Gelaterias (3)
27. Bar la Torre
28. Vernazza Wine Experience
29. Vineria Santa Marta
30. Cinque Terre Riviera Agency (Opéra Tickets)

future floods will be less destructive. They also installed nets above the town to protect it from landslides.

On the wall at the bend in the road, notice the **World Wars Monument**—dedicated to those killed in World Wars I and II. Not a family in Vernazza was spared.

Hikers take note: The **path to Corniglia** begins from here (behind and above the monument). You don't have to go far to find fine views over Vernazza's stony peninsula.

▶ *To see a more workaday part of Vernazza, head a couple of minutes uphill from here, to the...*

Top of Town

First you'll pass (on the left, at #7, with big brown garage doors and a *croce verde Vernazza* sign) the ambulance barn, where a group of volunteers is always on call for a dash to the hospital, 40 minutes away in La Spezia. Farther up, you'll come to a functional strip of modern apartment blocks facing the river. In this practical zone—the only place in town that allows cars—are a bank, the post office, a launderette, and the tourist hub bar/café called Il Pirata delle Cinque Terre. The parking lot fills a square called Fontana Vecchia, named for an "old fountain" that's so old, it's long gone. Shuttle buses run from here to hamlets and sanctuaries in the hills above.

Looming over this neighborhood is a terraced hill capped by the town cemetery (a steep hike) and, a climb beyond that, the town's sanctuary; for details on these hikes, see page 71.

► *The next leg of our walk heads downhill toward the harbor, following...*

Vernazza's "Main Street"

Just before the tracks, the town provides limited space for advertising for political parties. The walls under the tracks serve as a sort of community information center. The bulletin board on the right lists volunteers and when they are on call to drive the ambulance.

The second set of train tracks (nearer the harbor) was renovated to lessen disruptive noise (locals say it made no difference). At the base of the stairs a handy monitor displays up-to-the-minute schedules for arriving and departing trains (including any running late—*ritardo*).

On the left, just past the tracks, a giant poster shows photos of the 2011 flood *(alluvione)* and the shops it devastated. "The 25th of October" is a day that will live forever in this town's lore. Vernazza is built around one street—basically a lid over the stream in its ravine. On that fateful day, the surrounding hills acted like a funnel, directing flash-flood waters right through the middle of town. As you stroll from here to the harbor, imagine this street buried under 13 feet of mud. Every shop, restaurant, and hotel on the main drag had to be rewired, replumbed, and re-equipped.

You're now strolling through Vernazza's "commercial center": souvenir shops, wine shops, the Blue Marlin Bar (Vernazza's top nightspot), and so on. The small stone chapel with iron grillwork over the window (on the left) is the tiny Chapel of Santa Marta, where Mass is celebrated on special Sundays. Farther down, you'll walk by a *gelateria,* bakery, pharmacy, grocery, and another *gelateria.* There are plenty of fun and cheap food-to-go options here. While it's easy to get distracted by all the tourists, try to see through them to notice locals going about their business.

Stroll Vernazza's irresistible main street, and stop by its tranquil church.

▸ *On the left, in front of the second* gelateria, *a stone arch was blasted away by the 2011 flood. Scamper through the hole in the rock to reach Vernazza's shrinking...*

"New Beach"

This is where the town's stream used to hit the sea back in the 1970s. Older locals remember frolicking on a beach here when they were kids, but the constant, churning surf eventually eroded it all the way back to the cliff. When the 2011 flood hit, it blew out the passageway and deposited landslide material here from the hills above. In the flood's aftermath, Vernazza's main drag and harbor were filled with mud and silt. Workers used the debris to fill in even more of this beach. But as time goes on, the forces of nature are once again taking it away.

▸ *Back on the main drag, continue downhill to the...*

Harbor Square (Piazza Marconi) and Breakwater

Vernazza, with the Cinque Terre's only natural harbor, was established as the sole place boats could pick up the fine local wine. The two-foot-high square stone at the foot of the stairs (on the left) is marked *Sasso del Sego* (stone of tallow). Workers crushed animal flesh and fat in its basin to make tallow, which drained out from the tiny hole below. The tallow was then used to waterproof boats or wine barrels. Stonework is the soul of the region. Take some time to appreciate the impressive stonework of the restaurant interiors facing the harbor.

On the far side (behind Ristorante Pizzeria Vulnetia), peek into the tiny street with its commotion of arches. Vernazza's most characteristic side streets *(carugi)* lead up from here. The narrow stairs mark the beginning of the trail that leads up, up, up to the quintessential view of Vernazza (you could head up now for a quick photo op)—and, eventually, on to Monterosso.

Vernazza's harborfront **church** sits on the tiny piazza, decorated with a river-rock mosaic. This popular hangout spot is where the town's older ladies soak up the last bit of sun, and kids enjoy a patch of level ball field. The church is unusual for its east-facing entryway, rather than the more typical western orientation. With relative peace and prosperity in the 16th century, the townspeople doubled the size of the church, overtaking a little piazza that once faced the west facade.

From the square, use the "new" entry and climb the steps, noticing how high above the sea line the church must sit to stay dry. Inside, the lighter pillars in the back mark the 16th-century extension. Three historic portable crosses hanging on the walls are carried through town during religious processions. These are replicas of crosses that (locals like to believe) Vernazzan ships once carried on crusades to the Holy Land. The town priest, Don Giovanni, is popular—he stopped the church bells from ringing through the night (light sleepers rejoiced).

Colorful boats pulled up on Vernazza's harbor beach

The squat Belforte tower and castle tower overlook the sea.

▶ *Finish the rest of this tour seated out on the breakwater (perhaps with a glass of local white wine or something more interesting from a nearby bar—borrow the glass, they don't mind). Face the town, and see...*

The Harbor

In a moderate storm, you'd get soaked, as waves routinely crash over the *molo* (breakwater, built in 1972). Waves can rearrange the huge rocks—depositing them from the breakwater onto the piazza and its benches. Freak waves have even washed away tourists squinting excitedly into their cameras. (I've seen it happen.) In 2007, an American woman was swept away and killed by a rogue wave. Enjoy the waterfront piazza—carefully.

The train line (to your left) was constructed in 1874 to tie together a newly united Italy, linking Turin and Genoa with Rome. A second line (hidden in a tunnel at this point) was built in the 1920s. The yellow building alongside the tracks was Vernazza's first train station. Along the wall behind the tracks, you can see the four bricked-up alcoves where people once waited for trains. Notice the wonderful concrete sunbathing strip (and place for late-night privacy) laid below the tracks along the rocks.

Vernazza's fishing fleet is down to just a few boats with net spools, but Vernazzans are still more likely to own a boat than a car. Boats are moored on buoys, except in winter or when the red storm flag indicates bad seas (see the pole at the start of the breakwater). At these times, the boats are pulled up onto the square—which is usually reserved for restaurant tables. In the 1970s, tiny Vernazza had one of Italy's top water polo teams, and the harbor was their "pool." Later, when the league required a real pool, Vernazza dropped out.

The Castle (Castello Doria)

On the far right, the castle, which is now just stones and a grassy park with super views, still guards the town (€1.50, not covered by Cinque Terre park card, daily 9:30-20:00, summer until 21:00, closed Nov-March; from harbor, take stairs by Trattoria Gianni and follow *Ristorante al Castello* signs, tower is a few steps beyond). This was the town's watchtower back in pirate days, and a Nazi lookout in World War II. The castle tower looks new because it was rebuilt after the British bombed it to chase out the Germans.

The squat tower on the water, Ristorante Belforte, is a great spot for a glass of wine or a meal. From the breakwater, you could follow the rope to the restaurant and pop inside, past an actual submarine door. A photo of a major storm showing the entire tower under a wave (not uncommon in the winter) hangs near the bar.

The Town

Before the 12th century, pirates made the coast uninhabitable, so the first Vernazzans lived in the hills above (near the Reggio sanctuary). The town itself—and its towers, fortified walls, and hillside terracing—are mostly from

Vernazza's pastel palette is chosen by a commissioner of good taste.

the 12th through 15th century, when Vernazza was allied with the Republic of Genoa.

Vernazza has two halves. *Sciuiu* (Vernazzan dialect for "flowery") is the sunny side on the left, and *luvegu* (dank) is the shady side on the right. Houses below the castle were connected by an interior arcade—ideal for fleeing attacks.

The "Ligurian pastel" colors of the buildings are regulated by the regional government's commissioner of good taste. The square before you is locally famous for some of the area's finest restaurants. The big red central house—on the site where Genoan warships were built in the 12th century—used to be a guardhouse.

In the Middle Ages, there was no beach or square. The water went right up to the buildings, where boats would tie up, Venetian-style. Imagine what Vernazza looked like in those days, when it was the biggest and richest of the Cinque Terre towns. Buildings had a water gate (facing today's square) and a front door on the higher inland side. There was no pastel plaster—just fine stonework (traces of which survive above the Trattoria del Capitano). Apart from the added plaster, the general shape and size of the town has changed little in five centuries. Survey the windows and notice inhabitants quietly gazing back.

While the town has 1,500 residents in summer, only 500 stay here through the winter. Vernazza has accommodations for about 500 tourists.

Above the Town

The small, round tower above the red guardhouse—another part of the city fortifications—reminds us of the town's importance in the Middle Ages. Back then, Genoa's enemies (rival maritime republics, especially Pisa) were Vernazza's enemies. Bar la Torre, just above and beyond the tower, welcomes hikers who are finishing, starting, or simply contemplating the Corniglia-Vernazza hike, with great town views. That tower recalls a time when the entire town was fortified by a stone wall.

Vineyards fill the mountainside beyond the town. Notice the many terraces. For six centuries, the economy was based on wine and olive oil. Then came the 1980s—and the tourists. Locals turned to tourism to make a living, and stopped tending the land and vineyards. Terraces fell into disrepair, but it's the stonework of the terracing in the surrounding hills that helps prevent flooding—a lesson learned in the worst possible way in 2011.

Although many locals still maintain their small plots and proudly serve their family wines, the patchwork of vineyards is atomized and complex because of inheritance traditions. Historically, families divided their land among their children. Parents wanted each child to receive good land, though some lots were "kissed by the sun" while others were shady. Lots were split into increasingly tiny, unviable pieces, and many were eventually abandoned.

A single steel train line winds up the gully behind the tower. It is for the vintner's *trenino,* the little service train. Play "Where's *trenino?*" and see if you can find two trains. The vineyards once stretched as high as you can see, but since fewer people sweat in the fields these days, the most distant terraces have gone wild again.

The Church, School, and City Hall

Vernazza's Ligurian Gothic church, built with black stones quarried from Punta Mesco (the distant point behind you), dates from 1318. Note the gray stone that marks the church's 16th-century expansion. The gray-and-red house above the spire is the elementary school (about 25 children attend). Older students go to the "big city," La Spezia. The red building on the hill to the right of the schoolhouse, a former monastery, is the city hall. Vernazza and Corniglia function as one community. Through most of the 1990s, the local government was Communist. In 1999, residents elected a coalition of many parties working to rise above ideologies and simply make Vernazza a better place. That practical notion of government continues here today.

Finally, on the top of the hill, with the best view of all, is the town cemetery. It's only fair that hardworking Vernazzans—who spend their lives climbing up and down and up and down and up and down the hillsides that hem in their little town—are rewarded with a world-class view from their eternal resting place.

EXPERIENCES IN VERNAZZA

Hikes from Vernazza

For a rundown of ambitious hikes from Vernazza—including the main coastal trail to Corniglia and to Monterosso—see page 28. Here are some alternatives closer to town.

From Vernazza, you can hike in either direction for classic photo ops. Both hikes are steeply, but briefly, uphill (about 10 minutes to the best views and park ticket checkpoints).

Hike uphill from Vernazza (toward Monterosso or Corniglia) for classic views.

For the best light in the morning, follow the trail **toward Corniglia;** you'll twist up through vineyards to earn great views down over the stony back side of Vernazza's peninsula, with its round castle tower poking up and a Monterosso backdrop. The best views are from just before the national park ticket checkpoint. If you need a rewarding rest up here, Bar la Torre offers drinks with a grand view.

The trail **toward Monterosso** has the best light in the evening. From the harbor, you'll hike up through the steep and narrow *carugi* (alleys) before popping out on the trail above town. Follow this around the bluff, enjoying better and better views of Vernazza's tidy pastel harbor. The views are fine before the ticket booth, but even better after—if you don't want to buy a Cinque Terre park card, you can hike up here in the evening, after the park officially closes (typically around 19:00).

Hike to the Cemetery and Sanctuary: To hike up to Vernazza's sweet little **cemetery,** find the steep lane from the ravine at the top of town (mentioned on my "Vernazza Walk," earlier). From here, it's a 20-minute hike to the top. You'll find a peaceful world of lovingly tended family graves with stunning views over the Cinque Terre. Imagine the entire village sadly trudging up here during funerals. The cemetery is peaceful and evocative at sunset, when the fading light touches each crypt.

For a more ambitious hike, continue higher past the cemetery (a steep 30 minutes farther) to the town's sanctuary, **Madonna di Reggio.** Head straight up the ridge on the scenic, quiet trail #8/#508, passing the Stations of the Cross, to the sanctuary. For a much easier Reggio experience, you can ride the shuttle bus up to the sanctuary (departs from top of town, near post office), then hike down. Yet one more option: You can hike from Vernazza's sanctuary to Monterosso's sanctuary, then descend to Monterosso (see page 47).

Enjoy Vernazza's "new beach" and the sunning rocks at the harbor.

Beaches

The harbor's sandy cove has sunning rocks and showers by the breakwater. The sunbathing lane directly under the church has a shower. A ladder on the seaside of the breakwater aids deep-water swimmers. And, while it's getting smaller and rockier each year, Vernazza's "new beach" can be accessed through a hole halfway along the town's main drag.

Boat Rides

In addition to the regularly scheduled big boats that depart from Vernazza's harbor (see page 18), hiring your own boat can be handy for intertown transport. It's also a great way to escape the crowds and get a different angle on Cinque Terre splendor. From Vernazza, figure around €30 one-way to Monterosso, €40 to Manarola, or €50 to Riomaggiore (for up to six passengers in an outboard; a comfier 10-person boat costs more). Or hire a boat for a one-hour sightseeing cruise of the entire Cinque Terre (about €150); one popular stop is the tiny *acqua pendente* (waterfall) cove between Vernazza and Monterosso, which locals call their *laguna blu.*

At Vernazza's breakwater you'll find **Nord Est,** run by Vincenzo (with help from Cesare), the best-established option (mobile 338-700-0436, info@nordest-vernazza.com). **Vernazza Water Taxi,** run by Pietro, is another choice (mobile 338-911-3869, info@vernazzawatertaxi.it).

Shuttle Bus Joyride

For a cheap and scenic joyride, with a chance to chat about the region with friendly, English-speaking Mirco, Pietro, or Graziella, ride the ATC shuttle bus from the top of town (in front of the post office) to the sanctuaries and hamlets high in the hills—including the Reggio sanctuary (see "Hikes from Vernazza," on page 71) or the San Bernadino sanctuary

Vernazza's breakwater offers a shimmering view of the harbor at night.

above Corniglia—and back again (generally about 5/day, times are unpredictable—ask at train station TI or get schedule from bus driver).

Sustainable Tourism Activities

Save Vernazza, which began as a flood relief organization in 2011, has evolved into an all-purpose Vernazza advocacy group, with an emphasis on sustainable tourism. If you enjoy the Cinque Terre and would like to give something back, contact them to participate in a project designed to protect and promote Vernazza. Their "voluntourism" activities, scheduled regularly through the high season, include rebuilding terrace walls and harvesting grapes (reservations required, lunch and wine provided, generally 2/week late May-Oct 8:30-13:30, see website for schedule, www.savevernazza.com, workwithus@savevernazza.com, mobile 349-357-3572, Michelle and Ruth).

Wine Tasting

Vernazza Wine Experience hides out like a resort for jet-setters at the top of town just under the castle. Run by Alessandro, a sommelier, it's romantic, with mellow music, and a hardwood, ship-deck ambience. He enjoys explaining wines and the €15 small plates matched with them (like his meat-and-cheese plate served on a slab of olive tree). You'll pay €15 for three very different wines. He also has a €15 dessert wine/cheese/cookie deal. While the bill can add up, the quality is excellent and the view is unforgettable (cash only, daily 17:00-21:00, hike from harborfront and turn left before castle, Via S. Giovanni Battista 31, tel. 331-343-3801).

Vineria Santa Marta is simpler and mellower, with less scenery and pretense. At this wine shop/tasting bar with a stone terrace, brothers Wolfgang and Michael share their love of wine. A basic tasting of three local wines plus light snacks is €9 per person (also serves salads and *bruschette,* daily 9:30-20:30, above the little chapel on Via Roma—the main drag, tel. 0187-882-1084).

A Little Taste of Opera

My favorite Cinque Terre evenings are spent at Vernazza's summer opera. A big-name maestro from Lucca brings talented singers to town twice weekly to show off before an appreciative audience. Performances fill the small oratory tucked behind the town's big church (find the steps up and around, next to Ananasso Bar), which was beautifully restored for this purpose. Performances begin at 19:00 and last just over an hour—strategically timed to squeeze between a late-afternoon *aperitivo* on the harbor and a 20:30 dinner reservation (€13 in advance, €15 at the door, April-Oct Wed and Fri at 19:00 but confirm times locally, book tickets at Cinque Terre Riviera office at #24 on the main street—see map on page 62, tel. 0187-812-123, info@cinqueterreriviera.com).

NIGHTLIFE IN VERNAZZA

The town's nightlife centers on the bars on its waterfront piazza, which is the place to "see and be seen." The younger restaurant workers work hard throughout the tourist season, but they let loose after-hours and enjoy connecting with international visitors in the town's few nightspots (which must all close by midnight). For a more genteel option, consider an opera performance or a wine tasting (both described in the previous section). Or in the cool, calm evening, sit on the town's breakwater with a glass of wine and watch the phosphorescence in the waves.

The **Blue Marlin Bar** dominates the late-night scene with a mix of locals and tourists, home-cooked food until 23:00, good drinks, and occasional piano jam sessions. If you're young and hip, this is *the* place to hang out. If you play piano, you're welcome to contribute to the scene. **Ananasso Bar** offers early-evening happy-hour fun and cocktails *(aperitivi)* that both locals and visitors enjoy. Its harborfront tables get the last sunshine of the day. For more on these bars, see their listings under "Eating in Vernazza," later.

Really Late: A little cave on the beach just under the church lends itself to fun in the wee hours, when everything else is closed.

SLEEPING IN VERNAZZA

Vernazza lacks any real hotels, and almost all of my listings are *affittacamere* (private rooms for rent). I favor hosts who rent multiple rooms and have a proven track record of good communication (they speak just enough English, have email, and are reliable). But in many ways, the real Vernazza gems are stray single rooms with owners who have no interest in taking advance reservations. If you have the guts to just show up without a reservation and ask around, you may score a great deal. But—especially in busy times—it's safer to book ahead.

Most places accept only cash, promise free Wi-Fi (often spotty), and don't include breakfast unless noted (for suggestions, see "Eating in Vernazza," later). Some have killer views, and some come with lots of stairs. Expect noise at night: Trains tearing through, church bells (after 7:00 and before 22:00), crashing waves, cars in the upper town. Come to think of it, just pack earplugs.

While a few places have all their beds in one building, most have rooms scattered over town. Better-organized outfits have an informal "reception desk" (sometimes at a restaurant or other business) where you can check in. But many places have no reception at all. (The Vernazza map shows only the places that have a fixed address or reception office; if I mention "reception," you'll check in there, then continue on to your actual room.)

Because this can be confusing, I strongly recommend that you communicate your arrival time (by phone or email) and get clear instructions on where to meet the owner and pick up the keys. They'll usually offer to meet you at the train station—but only if they know when you're coming.

Rooms For Rent *(Affittacamere)*

Scattered Through the Town Center

The **Cinque Terre Riviera** agency, based in Vernazza, rents rooms here and throughout the region (www.cinqueterreriviera.com; see page 61).

$$$ La Malà is the town's jet-setter pad. Four crisp, pristine white rooms boast fancy-hotel-type extras and a shared seaview terrace. It's a climb—way up to the top of town—but they'll carry your bags to and from the station. Book early; this place fills up quickly (includes breakfast at a bar, family rooms, air-con, mobile 334-287-5718, www.lamala.it, info@lamala.it, charming Giamba and his mama, Armanda). They also rent the simpler **$ "Armanda's Room"** nearby—a great value, since you get Giamba's attention to detail and amenities without paying for a big view (includes simple breakfast, air-con).

$$ La Marina Rooms is run by hardworking Christian, who speaks English and happily meets guests at the station to carry bags. There are five well-tended (if slightly dated) units, most high above the main street: One single works as a (very) tight double, and three doubles share a fine oceanview terrace; they also have two **$$$** apartments—one with terrace and sea views, and the other on the harborfront square (mobile 338-476-7472, www.lamarinarooms.com, mapcri@yahoo.it).

$$ Emanuela Colombo has two rooms—one spacious and classy on the harbor square, the other a *molto* chic split-level apartment located on a quiet side street (sleeps up to four; Emanuela often works at the Bottega dell'Arte on the main street, tel. 339-834-2486, www.vacanzemanuela.it, manucap64@libero.it).

$$ Francamaria and her husband Andrea rent 10 sharp, comfortable, and creatively renovated rooms—all detailed on her website. Their reception desk is on the harbor square (on the ground floor at Piazza Marconi 30), but the rooms they manage are all over town (family rooms, some with air-con, spotty Wi-Fi, tel. 0187-812-002, mobile 328-711-9728, www.francamaria.com, info@francamaria.com).

$$ Vernazza Rooms, run by Daria Bianchi, Chiara, and Davide, rents 11 rooms: Four are above the Blue Marlin Bar looking down on the main street, and seven are a steep climb higher up, just under the city hall (big family apartments, ring bell at Via Roma 41—next to Blue Marlin Bar, a few with air-con and others with fans, limited English, mobile 338-581-4688 or 338-413-8696, www.vernazzarooms.com, info@vernazzarooms.com).

$$ Rosa Vitali rents two four-person apartments across from the pharmacy overlooking the main street (and beyond the train noise). One has a terrace and fridge (top floor); the other has windows and a full kitchen (family rooms, ring bell at Via Visconti 10—just before the tobacco shop near Piazza Marconi, tel. 0187-821-181, mobile 340-267-5009, www.rosacamere.it, rosa.vitali@libero.it).

$$ Maria Capellini rents two simple, clean rooms that face each other across the harbor; one is at ground level with a view, the other looks over a skinny street (family rooms, fans, mobile 338-436-3411, www.mariacapellini.com, mariacapellini@hotmail.it, kindly Maria and Giacomo).

$$ Martina Callo's four old-fashioned, spartan rooms overlook the harbor square; they're up plenty of steps near the silent-at-night church tower. While the rooms are simple, guests pay for and appreciate the views (family rooms, cheaper nonview room, air-con, ring bell at Piazza Marconi 26, tel. 0187-812-365, mobile 329-435-5344, www.roomartina.it, roomartina@roomartina.it).

$$ Nicolina Rooms consists of seven units in three different buildings. Two cheaper rooms are in the center over the pharmacy, up a few steep steps; another, pricier studio with a terrace is on a twisty lane above the harbor; and four more rooms are in a building beyond the church, with great views and church bells (all include breakfast, Piazza Marconi 29—check in at Pizzeria Vulnetia, tel. 0187-821-193, mobile 333-842-6879, www.camerenicolina.it, camerenicolina.info@cdh.it).

$ Rooms Francesca's two tidy rooms and one apartment hide out in the steep streets just below city hall (family rooms, check in at Enoteca Sciacchetrà at Via Roma 19, tel. 0187-821-112, www.5terre-vernazza.it, moggia.franco@libero.it; Francesca, Franco, and Sabine).

$ Ivo's Camere rents two tight but well-appointed rooms several flights of stairs above the main street (air-con, Via Roma 6, reception at Pizzeria Fratelli Basso—Via Roma 1, rooms across the street, mobile 333-477-5521, www.ivocamere.com, post@ivocamere.com).

$ Albergo Barbara rents nine basic-but-tidy, affordable top-floor rooms overlooking the square. Only a few rooms have real views; most have small windows and small views. It's run by English-speaking Giuseppe and his no-nonsense Swiss wife, Patricia (cheaper rooms with shared bathroom are a good value, more for views, lots of stairs, closed Dec-Feb, reserve online with credit card but pay cash, Piazza Marconi 30, tel. 0187-812-398, mobile 338-793-3261, www.albergobarbara.it, info@albergobarbara.it).

$ Memo Rooms rents three clean and spacious rooms overlooking the main street, in what feels like a miniature hotel. Enrica will meet you if you call upon arrival (Via Roma 15, try Enrica's mobile first at 338-285-2385, otherwise tel. 0187-812-360, www.memorooms.com, info@memorooms.com).

$ Monica Lercari rents several rooms with modern comforts, perched at the top of town (more for seaview terrace, includes breakfast, air-con, tel. 0187-812-296, mobile 320-025-4515, alcastellovernazza@yahoo.it). Monica and her husband, Massimo, run the recommended Ristorante al Castello, in the old castle tower overlooking town.

More Options: $ Capitano Rooms (3 rooms several flights of stairs above main drag, fans; ask for Julia, Paolo, or Barbara at Trattoria del Capitano restaurant on main square at Piazza Marconi 21; tel. 0187-812-201, www.tavernavernazza.com, info@tavernavernazza.com); **$$ Eva's Rooms** (3 rooms on main street, air-con, train noise, meet at boutique at Via Roma 68, tel. 334-798-6500, www.evasrooms.it, evasrooms@yahoo.it); **$$ Rooms Elisabetta** (3 tight, recently renovated, casually run rooms at the tip-top of town with Vernazza's ultimate 360-degree roof terrace—come here for the views; family rooms, fans, partway up Corniglia path at Via Carattino 62, mobile 347-451-1834, www.elisabettacarro.it, carroelisabetta@hotmail.com, Elisabetta); and **$$ Manuela Moggia** (family rooms, more for room with kitchen or view, some behind train station at Via Gavino 22, tel. 0187-812-397, mobile 333-413-6374, www.manuela-vernazza.com, info@manuela-vernazza.com).

In the Inland Part of Town

Above the Train Station: $$ Giuliano Basso's four carefully crafted, well-appointed rooms form a cozy little compound on the green hillside just above town, straddling a ravine among orange trees. Giuliano—the town's last stone-layer—proudly built the place himself (2 rooms have air-con, more train noise than others; follow the main road up above the station, take the ramp up toward Corniglia just before Pensione Sorriso, follow the path, and watch for a sharp left turn toward the US and California flags; mobile 333-341-4792, www.cdh.it/giuliano, giuliano@cdh.it).

In the Ravine at the Top of Town: These practical options are a five-minute, gently uphill stroll behind the train station. While this functional zone is less atmospheric and feels less central, it does provide easier access (with fewer steep stairs). There's no train or church-bell noise—the constant soundtrack is Vernazza's gurgling river—but there can be traffic noise. Il Pirata delle Cinque Terre is the neighborhood hub (offering breakfast, tourist bonding, and Wi-Fi), and Vernazza's launderette is right next door.

$$ Camere Fontana Vecchia, run by Annamaria, is the best choice here, with eight bright and cheery rooms overlooking the ravine and its rushing river (cheaper room with shared bath, more for terrace, Via Gavino 15, tel. 0187-821-130, mobile 333-454-9371, www.cinqueterrecamere.com, m.annamaria@libero.it). **$$ Tonino Basso** has four overpriced but colorful rooms in a drab, elevator-equipped, modern apartment block (air-con, Via Gavino 34, mobile 339-761-1651, www.toninobasso.com, Alessandra).

$ La Rosa dei Venti ("The Compass Rose"), run by Giuliana Basso, houses three airy, good-value rooms in her childhood home, on the third floor of an apartment building (call to arrange meeting time, air-con, Via Gavino 19, mobile 333-762-4679, www.larosadeiventi-vernazza.it, info@larosadeiventi-vernazza.it).

Guesthouses *(Pensiones)*

These guesthouses have many rooms and something resembling a reception desk, but still, I'd consider them a last resort. They're overpriced and lack the thoughtful touches of a Vernazzan who oversees just a couple of private rooms.

$$$ Gianni Franzi, a busy restaurant on the harbor square, rents 25 small rooms scattered across three buildings a hundred tight, winding stairs above the harbor square. Some rooms (including a few cheaper ones with shared bathrooms) are funky and decorated à la shipwreck, with tiny balconies and grand sea views; the comfy, newer rooms lack views. All rooms have access to a super-scenic cliff-hanging guests' garden (where breakfast is served mid-April-mid-Oct). Steely Marisa requires check-in before 16:00 or a phone call to explain when you're coming. Emanuele, Simona, Caterina, and the staff speak a little English (RS%, closed Jan-Feb, Piazza Marconi 1, tel. 0187-812-228, tel. 0187-821-003, mobile 393-9008-155, www.giannifranzi.it, info@giannifranzi.it). Pick up your keys at Gianni Franzi restaurant on the harbor square (on Wed, when the restaurant is closed, call ahead to make other arrangements).

$$$ Pensione Sorriso rents 13 decent but pricey rooms just up the road from the train station (cheaper rooms with shared bath and no air-con, breakfast extra, train noise, closed Nov-March, Via Gavino 4, tel. 0187-812-224, www.pensionesorriso.com, info@pensionesorriso.com, Francesca and Aldo).

EATING IN VERNAZZA

Breakfast

If you're seeking a real breakfast, you have five basic options: Blue Marlin and Capitano for their extensive menus; Il Pirata for sugary stuff and a lively welcome; Ananasso for coffee and a sweet roll on the harborfront; or any bakery for picnic goodies.

$$ Blue Marlin Bar (midtown, just below the train station) serves a good array of clearly priced à la carte breakfast items including eggs and bacon (8:30-11:30)—figure around €10 total with a *caffè lungo.* It's run by Massimo and Carmen with the capable assistance of Jeff, an American. If you're awaiting a train any time of day, the Blue Marlin's outdoor seating—within view of the tracks—beats the platform (Thu-Tue 7:00-24:00, closed Wed).

$$ Trattoria del Capitano offers outdoor seating on the harbor, as well as cozy spots inside the restaurant. You can order single items (€6 egg

Twin brothers run the popular Il Pirata delle Cinque Terre café.

dishes including focaccia and small salad) or opt for the €12 full-and-filling breakfast (Wed-Mon from 8:00, closed Tue except in Aug).

$ Il Pirata delle Cinque Terre is located in the workaday zone at the parking lot at the top of town. The fun, playful service of the dynamic duo Gianluca and Massimo (hardworking Sicilian twins, a.k.a. the Cannoli brothers) makes up for the lack of a view. Massimo is a likeable loudmouth, while Gianluca is a pastry artist. Their sweet pastry breakfasts include an array of treats like *panzerotto* (with ricotta, cinnamon, and vanilla) and hot cheese and pesto bruschetta. They pride themselves on not serving bacon and eggs, since "this is Italy." While the atmosphere of the place feels more like suburban Milan, it has a curious charisma among its customers (daily 6:30-24:00, Via Gavino 36, tel. 0187-812-047).

$$ Ananasso Bar has a youthful energy and great location with little tables right on the harbor. They offer toasted *panini,* pastries, and designer cappuccino. You can eat a bit cheaper at the bar (you're welcome to picnic on the nearby bench or seawall rocks with a Mediterranean view) or enjoy the best-situated tables in town (Fri-Wed 8:00-late, closed Thu).

Picnic Breakfast: Drop by one of Vernazza's many little bakeries, focaccia shops, or grocery stores to assemble a breakfast to eat on the breakwater. Top it off with a coffee in a nearby bar.

Lunch and Dinner

Vernazza's restaurants take pride in their cooking. Wander around at about 20:00 and compare the ambience, but don't wait too late to eat—many kitchens close at 22:00. If you dine in Vernazza but are staying in another town, be sure to check train schedules before sitting down to eat, as evening trains run less frequently with gaps in the schedule. To get an outdoor table on summer weekends, reserve ahead. Harborside restaurants and bars are easygoing. You're welcome to grab a cup of coffee or glass of wine and disappear somewhere on the breakwater, returning your glass when you're done.

Harborside

$$$ Gianni Franzi is an old standby for well-prepared seafood and pastas. Emanuele, Alessandro, and their crew provide steady, reliable, and friendly service. The outdoor seating is partially tucked under an arcade, while the indoor setting is big, open, and classy (check their *menù cucina* *tipica Vernazza,* Thu-Tue 12:00-15:00 & 19:00-22:00, closed Wed except in Aug, tel. 0187-812-228).

$$$ Trattoria del Capitano feels unpretentious and serves a short menu of straightforward local dishes, including *spaghetti allo scoglio*—pasta entangled with various types of seafood, and *grigliata mista*—a mix of seasonal Mediterranean fish (Wed-Mon 12:00-22:00, closed Tue and Dec-Jan, tel. 0187-812-201, hardworking Paolo and Barbara speak English).

$$$ Ristorante Pizzeria Vulnetia has a nautical, jovial atmosphere. Like the others listed here, it serves regional specialties; but unlike the others, it also dishes up affordable pizzas—making this a good choice for a group with differing tastes, those on a budget, and families (Tue-Sun 12:00-22:00, closed Mon, Piazza Marconi 29, tel. 0187-821-193, Giuliano and Tullio).

$$ Pizzeria Baia Saracena ("Saracen Bay") is the budget option on the harbor, serving forgettable pizza and pastas out on the breakwater. Eat here not for high cuisine, but for a memorable atmosphere at reasonable prices (Sat-Thu 10:30-22:00, closed Fri, tel. 0187-812-113, Luca).

$$$$ Gambero Rosso rounds out the options on the harbor. It's the priciest place on the square, but—ever since it was sold to a big-city restaurateur who runs it from afar—the quality can be hit-or-miss. Still, it has a fine interior and great outdoor tables (Fri-Wed 12:00-15:00 & 19:00-21:30, closed Thu and Dec-Feb, Piazza Marconi 7, tel. 0187-812-265).

Above the Harbor, by the Castle

$$$$ Ristorante Belforte serves a fine blend of traditional and creative cuisine, including a hearty *zuppa Michela* (€30/person for a boatload of seafood, 2-person minimum), fishy *spaghetti alla Bruno, trofie al pesto* (hand-rolled noodles with pesto), and classic *antipasto misto di pesce*—an assortment of fish (€20/person for 5 plates; 2-person minimum). From the breakwater, follow either set of stairs that lead up from the harbor. You'll find a web of tables embedded in four levels of the old castle. For the ultimate seaside perch, call and reserve one of the tables on the *terrazza con vista* (view terrace); for a really special meal, request the "lovers' table" on its own little terrace. Most of Belforte's seating is outdoors—if the weather's bad, the interior can get crowded (Wed-Mon 12:00-15:00 & 19:00-22:00, closed Tue and Nov-March, tel. 0187-812-222, Michela).

$$$ Ristorante al Castello is run by gracious and English-speaking Monica, her husband Massimo, and their sometimes-gruff staff. Hike high above town to just below the castle for commanding views. Reserve one of the dozen romantic cliff-side seaview tables for two—some of the tables snake around the castle, where you'll feel like you're eating all alone with the Mediterranean. Monica offers a free *sciacchetrà* or *limoncello* with biscotti with this book by request (Thu–Tue 12:00–15:00 & 19:00–22:00, closed Wed and Nov–April, tel. 0187-812-296).

On or near the Main Street

Several of Vernazza's inland eateries manage to compete without the harbor ambience but with slightly cheaper prices.

$$ Trattoria da Sandro, on the main drag, mixes quality Genovese and Ligurian cuisine with friendly service and can be a peaceful alternative to the harborside scene. The family proudly maintains its cultural traditions and dishes up award-winning stuffed mussels (Wed-Mon 12:00-15:00 & 18:30-22:00, closed Tue, Via Roma 62, tel. 0187-812-223, Argentina and Alessandro).

$$ Antica Osteria il Baretto is another solid bet for homey, reasonably priced traditional cuisine, run by Simone and Jenny. As it's off the harbor and less glitzy than the others, it's favored by locals who prefer less noisy English while they eat great homemade fare. Sitting deep in their interior can be a tranquil escape (Tue-Sun 12:00-22:00, closed Mon, indoor and outdoor seating in summer, Via Roma 31, tel. 0187-812-381).

Other Eating Options

$$ Blue Marlin Bar (on the main street and described under "Breakfast," earlier) busts out of the Vernazzan-cuisine rut with a short, creative menu of more casual dishes (pizzas, pastas, and *secondi*). It's a good choice if you want to just grab some reliable food rather than dine. Locals enjoy a meal here when they don't feel like cooking at home (closed Wed).

$$ Il Pirata delle Cinque Terre, an endearing tourist trap, is best for breakfast but also attracts many travelers for lunch and dinner. Come here not for the cuisine or the ambience, but for a memorable evening with the Cannoli twins, who entertain while they serve. The menu (pastas and salads) is aimed squarely at American tourists' taste buds (lunch daily from 12:00, dinner from 18:00, good Sicilian slushies, at the top of town; see complete listing under "Breakfast," earlier).

Pizzerias, Sandwiches, and Groceries: Vernazza's main-street eateries offer a fine range of quick meals. Two **pizzerias** mostly do takeout, but they'll let you sit and eat for the same cheap price. One has tables on the street, and the other, called Ercole, hides a tiny terrace and a few tables out back. **Forno Bakery** has good focaccia and veggie tarts (at #5), and several bars sell sandwiches and pizza by the slice. **Pino's grocery store** also makes inexpensive sandwiches to order (generally Mon-Sat 8:00-13:00 & 17:00-19:30, closed Sun). **Lunch Box** is a notch above, with panini, salads, and fresh fruit juices. If it's not too busy, they invite you to assemble your own salad (or juice) from a long list of ingredients (daily 8:00-21:00, shorter hours off-season, Via Roma 34, mobile 338-908-2841, Stefano).

Gelato: The town has three gelato shops. On the harbor, the aptly named **Gelateria Il Porticciolo** ("Marina") is arguably the best; they use fresh ingredients to create intense flavors (try their *cannella*—cinnamon, or *nocciola*—hazelnut). **Gelateria Vernazza,** near the top of the main street, takes its gelato seriously, occasionally flirting with creative ingredients (soy) and flavors (*riso*—rice, and ricotta and fig). **Gelateria Amore Mio** (midtown) used to be Gelateria Stalin, founded in 1968 by a pastry chef with that unfortunate name; now it's run by his niece Sonia and nephew Francesco, with great people-watching tables but the least exciting gelato in town.

MENU
Acciughe
Insalate
Pizze
Focaccia
Panini
Bruschette
Torte di Verdura

Corniglia

If you think of the Cinque Terre as the Beatles, Corniglia is Ringo. This tiny, sleepy town—the only one of the five not directly on the water—owns a laid-back main square. According to a (likely fanciful) local legend, the town was originally settled by a Roman farmer who named it for his mother, Cornelia (how Corniglia is pronounced). Its ancient residents produced a wine so widely exported that—some say—vases have been found at Pompeii stamped with the town name. Wine remains Corniglia's lifeblood today. Sample some when you're in town.

Less visited than the other Cinque Terre towns, Corniglia has fewer tourists, cooler temperatures, a few restaurants, a windy overlook on its promontory, and plenty of private rooms for rent (ask at any bar or shop, no cheaper than other towns).

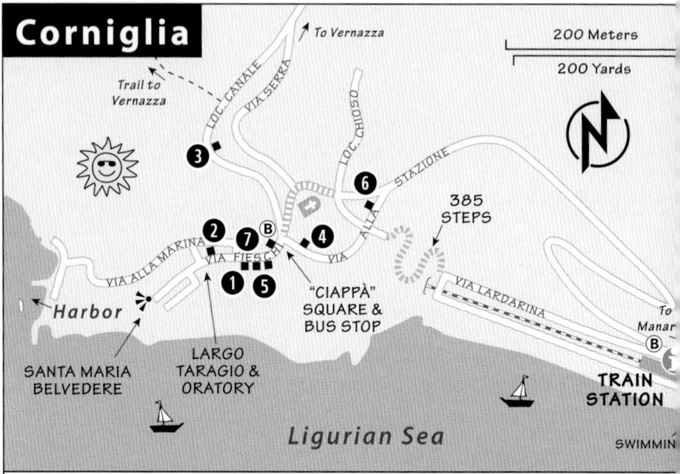

1. Pan e Vin Bar (Ricci Rooms Check-In)
2. Il Carugio Rooms, KmO Shop & Butiega Shop
3. Villa Cecio Rooms
4. Corniglia Hostel
5. Osteria Mananan & Enoteca il Pirùn
6. La Posada Ristorante
7. Gelateria

Corniglia has rocky sea access below its train station (toward Manarola). The beach here has all been washed away—but look for signs that say *al mare* or *Marina,* where a trail leads from the town center steeply down to sunning rocks (with a shower).

Hill-capping Corniglia is connected with its train station far below by a long set of stairs, and much easier, a hardworking little shuttle bus. Its reliable schedule is posted both at the station and in the town.

Because of the steep distance between the town and its station, and the lack of a boat dock, Corniglia is a less convenient home base for town-hopping.

ORIENTATION TO CORNIGLIA

Tourist Information

A TI/park information office is at the train station (likely daily 8:00-20:00, shorter hours off-season).

Arrival in Corniglia

By Train: From the station far below town, you can take a footpath zigzagging up 385 steps (and nearly that many switchbacks) to the town in about 20 minutes. If you'd rather not walk, hop on the tiny shuttle bus—generally timed to meet arriving trains—which connects the station with Corniglia's main square, the start of my short self-guided walk (1-2/hour).

If leaving Corniglia by train, review the shuttle schedule and time your visit to catch the bus down to conveniently arrive at the station in time for your departure.

By Car: Only residents can park on the main road between the recommended Villa Cecio and the point where the steep switchback staircase meets the road. Beyond that area, parking is €2/hour (up to €10/day). All parking areas are within an easy and fairly level walk of the town center.

Nearly 400 steps link Corniglia's town to its train station.

CORNIGLIA WALK

We'll explore this tiny town—population 240—and end at a scenic viewpoint. This self-guided walk might take up to 30 minutes or more... but only if you let yourself browse, sample the wine, or lick a gelato cone.

▸ *Begin near the shuttle bus stop located at a...*

Town Square

The gateway to this community is "Ciappà" square, with an ATM, old wine press, and bus stop. The Cinque Terre's designation as a national park sparked a revitalization of the town. Corniglia's young generation is more likely now to stay put, rather than migrate into big cities the way locals did in the past.

▸ *Look for the arrow pointing to the centro. Stroll along Via Fieschi, the spine of Corniglia. In the fall, the smell of grapes (on their way to becoming wine) wafts from busy cellars. Along this main street, you'll see...*

Corniglia's Enticing Shops

As you enter Via Fieschi, a trio of neighboring, fiercely competitive gelato shops jockey for your business. Don't settle for second-best: My favorite is the last one you come to (at #74, on the right), **Alberto's Gelateria.** Before ordering, get a free taste of Alberto's *miele di Corniglia,* made from local honey; he's also proud of his basil flavor, and his lemon slush *(granita)* takes pucker to new heights.

Farther along, on the left, **Enoteca il Pirùn**—named for a type of oddly shaped old-fashioned wine pitcher designed to aerate the wine and give the alcohol more kick as you squirt it into your mouth—is located in a cool cantina at Via Fieschi 115. Sample some local wines (small tastes generally free, €3/glass). If you order wine to drink from the *pirùn,* Mario will give you a bib. While this is a practical matter (rookies are known to dribble), it also makes a nice souvenir.

A bit farther along are two interesting shops—particularly for picnic shoppers. On the left, at #151, Franco's shop **Km0** ("kilometer zero") focuses on locally sourced wines and beers from the Cinque Terre, and meats and cheeses from within a few miles of here (*panini* and smoothies, daily 10:00-21:00, closed Tue off-season). They've even reclaimed some

Glimpse slice-of-life scenes on a walk through Corniglia.

farmland on the adjacent hill (visible from just outside the shop) to grow their own produce.

Across the street, at the **Butiega** shop (#142), Vincenzo sells organic local specialties (daily 8:00-19:30). For picnickers, they offer €3 made-to-order ham-and-cheese sandwiches and a fun *antipasti misti* (priced by weight). Veronica prepares specialties such as pesto daily in the shop's tiny kitchen. You'll find good places to picnic farther along on this walk.

▶ *Following Via Fieschi, you'll end up at the mellow...*

Main Square

On Largo Taragio, tables from two bars and a trattoria spill around a WWI memorial and the town's old well. It once piped in natural spring water from the hillside to locals living without plumbing. What looks like a church is the Oratory of Santa Caterina. (An oratory is a kind of spiritual clubhouse for a service group doing social work in the name of the Catholic Church.) Up the stairs behind the oratory, you'll find a clearing that children have made into a soccer field. The stone benches and viewpoint make this a peaceful place for a picnic (less crowded than the end-of-town viewpoint, described next).

▶ *Opposite the oratory, notice how steps lead steeply down (in 5 minutes) on Via alla Marina to sunning rocks, a shower, and a small deck (with a treacherous entry into the water). From the square, continue up Via Fieschi to the...*

End-of-Town Viewpoint

The Santa Maria Belvedere, named for a church that once stood here, marks the scenic end of Corniglia. This is a super picnic spot. From here, look high to the west (right), where the village and sanctuary of San Bernardino straddle a ridge (accessible by shuttle bus from Monterosso or a long uphill hike from Vernazza). Below is the tortuous harbor, where locals hoist their boats onto the cruel rocks.

EXPERIENCES IN CORNIGLIA

Hikes from Corniglia

From Corniglia, you can hike on the coastal trail to **Vernazza,** or—if it's open—to **Manarola.** Also consider the challenging but rewarding "high road" to **Manarola via Volastra.** For details on these options, see "Hiking the Cinque Terre" on page 23.

SLEEPING IN CORNIGLIA

Corniglia is riddled with humble places that charge too much (given its harborless location) and some hosts who have a limited ability to converse with tourists. It's almost never full.

$ Cristiana Ricci communicates well and is reliable, renting three small, clean, and peaceful rooms—one with a terrace and sweeping view—just inland from the bus stop (family rooms, check in at Pan e Vin bar at Via Fieschi 123, mobile 338-937-6547, cri_affittacamere@virgilio.it). She also rents three big, modern apartments.

$ Il Carugio has nine modern, fresh, sunny rooms right in the center of the village, most with sea views. The communal rooftop terrace offers a commanding view of the coast (air-con, no breakfast but small self-service kitchen, free parking, free self-serve laundry, tel. 0187-812-293, mobile 335-175-7946 or 339-228-3803, www.ilcarugiodicorniglia.com, info@ilcarugiodicorniglia.com, Lidia). They also have a two-bedroom apartment facing the main square.

$ Villa Cecio (pronounced "chay-choh") feels like an abandoned hotel. They offer eight well-worn rooms on the outskirts of town, with saggy beds and little character. Some rooms have great views, and three have terraces—worth requesting when you check in. All rooms share a big rooftop view terrace (breakfast extra, four rooms have air-con, on main road 200 yards toward Vernazza at Via Serra 58, tel. 0187-812-043, mobile

366-285-1178, www.cecio5terre.com, info@cecio5terre.com, Giacinto). They also rent eight similar rooms in an annex on the square where the bus stops.

¢ Corniglia Hostel, the town's former schoolhouse, rents 24 beds in a pastel-yellow municipal building up some steps from the square where the bus stops (find the entrance at the back of the building). The playground in front is often busy with happy kids. Despite its strict and institutional atmosphere, the hostel's prices, central location, and bright, clean rooms ensure its popularity. Its hotelesque double rooms are open to anyone (breakfast extra, office open 7:00-13:00 & 15:00-1:30 in the morning, dorms closed 10:30-15:00, private rooms closed 13:00-15:00, 1:30 curfew, air-con, self-serve laundry, Via alla Stazione 3, tel. 0187-812-559, www.ostellocorniglia.com, ostellocorniglia@gmail.com, Andrea, Alessandro, and Elisabetta).

EATING IN CORNIGLIA

The typical array of pizzerias, *focaccerie,* and *alimentari* (grocery stores) line the narrow main drag. I've highlighted a few places for a quick bite on my self-guided walk. For a full, sit-down meal, consider one of these restaurants:

$$ Osteria Mananan—between the Ciappà bus stop and the main square at Via Fieschi 117—serves what many consider the best food in town in its small, stony, elegant interior (Tue-Sun 12:30-14:30 & 19:30-22:00, closed Mon, no outdoor seating, tel. 0187-821-166).

$$ Enoteca il Pirùn, next door on Via Fieschi, has a small restaurant above the wine bar, where Mario serves typical local dishes (daily 12:00-16:00 & 19:30-23:30, tel. 0187-812-315).

$$ La Posada Ristorante offers dinner in a garden under trees, overlooking the Ligurian Sea. To get here, stroll out of town to the top of the stairs that lead down to the station (daily 12:00-16:00 & 19:00-23:00, tel. 0187-821-174, mobile 338-232-5734).

Manarola

Mellow Manarola fills a ravine, bookended by its wild little harbor to the west and a diminutive hilltop church square inland to the east. Manarola is exceptional for being unexceptional: While Vernazza is prettier, Monterosso glitzier, Riomaggiore bigger, and Corniglia more rustic, Manarola hits a fine balance, giving it the "just right" combination of Cinque Terre qualities. Perhaps that's why it's a favorite among savvy Europeans seeking a relatively untrampled home base. The touristy zone squeezed between the cement-encased train tracks and the harbor can be stressfully congested, but head just a few steps uphill and you can breathe again. Popular with hikers, it may be the Cinque Terre's steepest town—but the higher you go, the less crowded it gets, culminating in the essentially tourist-free residential zone that clings to the ridge.

Manarola, whose hillsides are blanketed with vineyards, also provides the easiest access to the Cinque Terre's remarkable dry-stone terraces. The trail ringing the town's cemetery peninsula, adjacent to the main harbor, provides some of the most strikingly beautiful town views anywhere in the region (best light late in the day). For a look at all the facets of this delightful town, follow my gentle self-guided stroll from the harbor up through town to the vineyards, and a stunning Mediterranean viewpoint.

ORIENTATION TO MANAROLA

Tourist Information

The TI/national park information office is in the train station (likely daily 8:00-19:30, shorter hours off-season).

Arrival in Manarola

By Train: From the station, to reach Manarola's elevated square, you'll walk through a 200-yard-long tunnel that's lined with interesting photos. (During WWII air raids, these tunnels provided refuge and a safe place for rattled villagers to sleep.) To reach the busy harbor—with touristy restaurants, boat dock, and the start of my self-guided walk—cross the square, then go down the other side. To reach the town, hilltop church, and vineyard strolls, turn right.

The ATC **shuttle bus** runs from near the post office (halfway up Manarola's main street), stopping first at the parking lots above town, and then going all the way up to Volastra (about 2/hour except for afternoon breaks).

By Car: Unless you're sleeping here, you're not allowed to drive into Manarola. Park your car in one of the two lots just before town (€2/hour),

Manarola has picturesque perches and an artsy square.

then walk down the road to the church; from there, it's an easy downhill walk to the main piazza, train-station tunnel (and trailhead for the Via dell'Amore to Riomaggiore), and harbor (the start of my self-guided walk)—or you can wait for the shuttle bus. If you're sleeping here, ask your hotelier for parking advice.

MANAROLA WALK

From the harbor, this 45-minute self-guided circular walk shows you the town and surrounding vineyards and ends at a fantastic viewpoint, perfect for a picnic.

▸ *Start down at the waterfront. Belly up to the wooden banister overlooking the rocky harbor, between the two restaurants.*

The Harbor

Manarola is tiny and picturesque, a tumble of buildings bunny-hopping down its ravine to the fun-loving waterfront. The breakwater—which attempts to make this jagged harbor a bit less dangerous—was built just over a decade ago. Notice how the I-beam crane launches the boats (which must be pulled ashore when bad weather is expected, to avoid being smashed or swept away).

Facing the water, look up to the right, at the hillside Punta Bonfiglio cemetery and park. The trail running around the base of the point—where this walk ends—offers magnificent views back on this part of town.

The town's swimming hole is just below you. Manarola has no sand, but offers the best deep-water swimming in the area. The first "beach" has a shower, ladder, and wonderful rocks. The second has tougher access and no shower, but feels more remote and pristine (follow the paved path toward Corniglia, just around the point). For many, the tricky access makes this "beach" dangerous.

▸ *Go inland up the town's main drag—you'll climb a steep ramp to reach Manarola's "new" square, which covers the train tracks.*

Piazza Capellini

Built in 2004, this square is an all-around great idea, giving the town a safe, fun zone for kids. Locals living near the tracks also enjoy a little less train

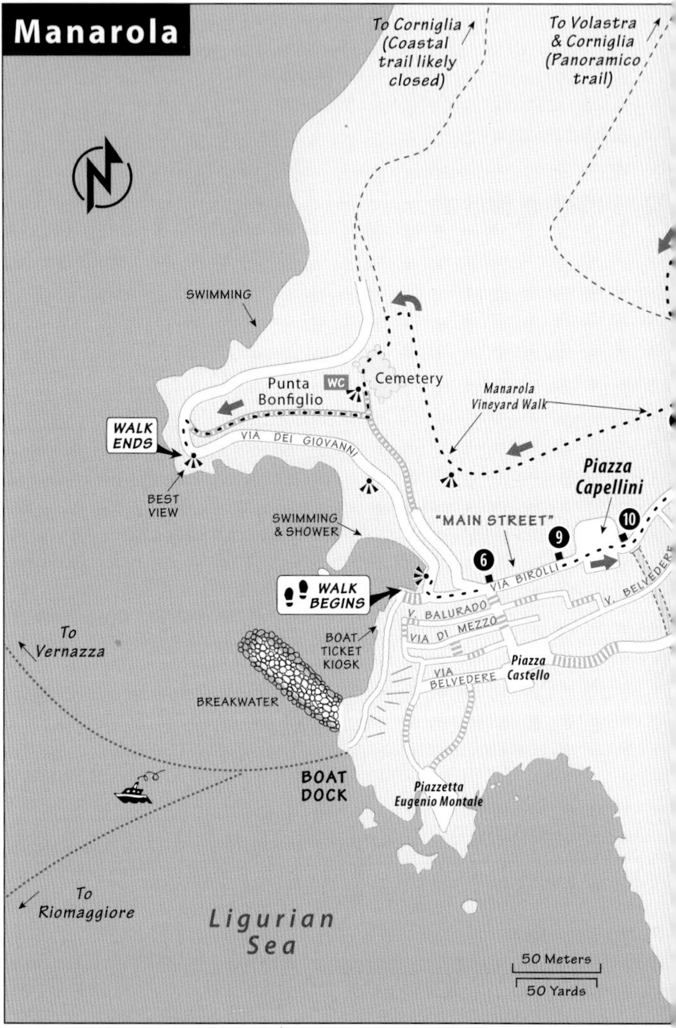
Manarola
To Corniglia (Coastal trail likely closed)
To Volastra & Corniglia (Panoramico trail)
SWIMMING
Punta Bonfiglio
WC
Cemetery
Manarola Vineyard Walk
WALK ENDS
VIA DEI GIOVANNI
BEST VIEW
Piazza Capellini
SWIMMING & SHOWER
"MAIN STREET"
6
9
10
VIA BIROLLI
V. BELVEDERE
WALK BEGINS
V. BALURADO
VIA DI MEZZO
To Vernazza
BOAT TICKET KIOSK
Piazza Castello
VIA BELVEDERE
BREAKWATER
BOAT DOCK
Piazzetta Eugenio Montale
To Riomaggiore
Ligurian Sea
50 Meters
50 Yards

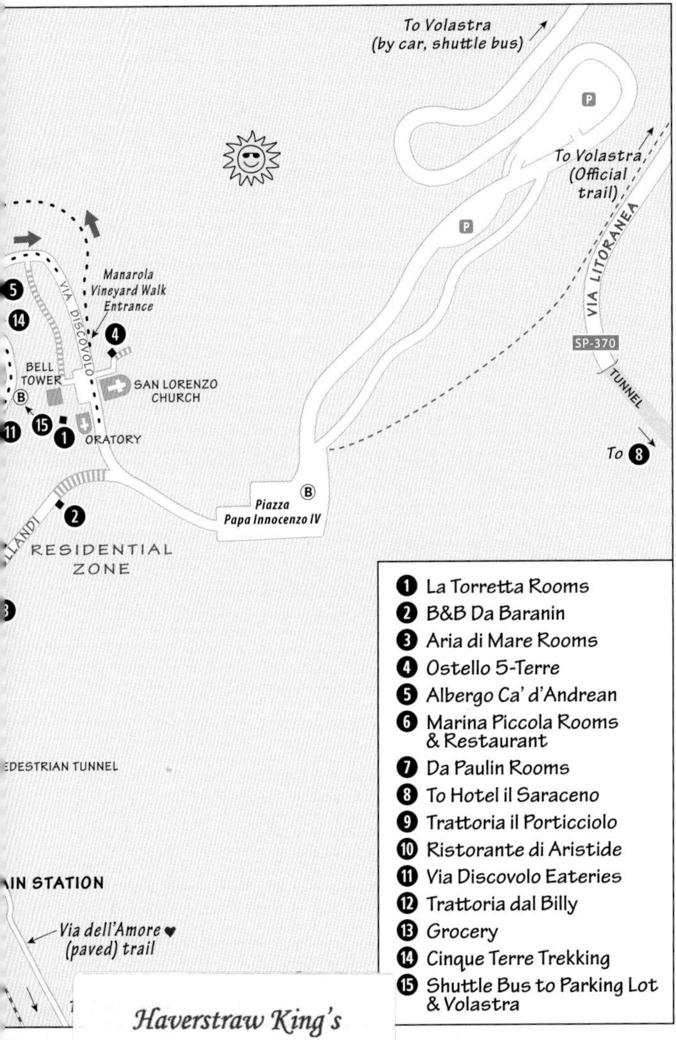

1. La Torretta Rooms
2. B&B Da Baranin
3. Aria di Mare Rooms
4. Ostello 5-Terre
5. Albergo Ca' d'Andrean
6. Marina Piccola Rooms & Restaurant
7. Da Paulin Rooms
8. To Hotel il Saraceno
9. Trattoria il Porticciolo
10. Ristorante di Aristide
11. Via Discovolo Eateries
12. Trattoria dal Billy
13. Grocery
14. Cinque Terre Trekking
15. Shuttle Bus to Parking Lot & Volastra

noise. Check out the mosaic in the middle of the square, which depicts the varieties of local fish in colorful enamel. The recommended Ristorante di Aristide has an inviting terrace right on the square.

▸ *Go down the stairs at the upper end of the square. On your right, notice the tunnel that leads to Manarola's train station (and the Via dell'Amore trailhead). But for now, head up...*

Via Discovolo

Manarola's sleepy main street twists up through town, lined by modest shops and filled with pooped hikers. About 100 yards up, just before the road bends sharply right, watch (on the right) for a waterwheel. This recalls the origin of the town's name—local dialect for "big wheel" (one of many possible derivations). Mills like this once powered the local olive oil industry. As you continue up (all the way to the church), you'll still hear the rushing waters of Manarola's stream. Like the streams in Riomaggiore, Monterosso, and Vernazza, Manarola's rivulet was covered over by a modern sewage system after World War II. Before that time, romantic bridges arched over its ravine. You can peek below the concrete street in several places to see the stream surging below your feet.

Across the street from the waterwheel and a bit farther up, notice the **Cinque Terre Trekking** shop on your left, which outfits hikers with both information and gear (see page 103 for details).

▸ *Keep switchbacking up until you come to the square at the...*

Top of Manarola

The square is faced by a church, an oratory—now a religious and community meeting place—and a bell tower, which served as a watchtower when pirates raided the town (the cupola was added once the attacks ceased). Behind the church is Manarola's well-run youth hostel, originally the church's schoolhouse. To the right of the oratory, a stepped lane leads to Manarola's sizable tourist-free residential zone.

Check out the **church.** According to the white marble plaque in its facade, the Parish Church of St. Lawrence (San Lorenzo) dates from "MCCCXXXVIII" (1338). Step inside to see two altarpiece paintings from the unnamed Master of the Cinque Terre, the only painter of any note from this region (left wall and above main altar). While the style is Gothic, the work dates from the late 15th century, long after Florence had entered the Renaissance. Note the humble painted stone ceiling, which replaced the wooden original

Enjoy the views along Manarola's vineyard walk.

in the 1800s. It features Lawrence, patron saint of the Cinque Terre, with his grill, the symbol of his martyrdom (he was roasted on it).

► *With the bell tower on your left, head about 20 yards back down the main street below the church and find a wooden railing. It marks the start of a delightful stroll around the high side of town, and back to the seafront. This is the beginning of the...*

Manarola Vineyard Walk

Don't miss this experience. Simply follow the wooden railing, enjoying lemon groves and wild red valerian (used for insomnia since the days of the Romans). Along the path, which is primarily flat, you'll get a close-up look at the region's famous dry-stone walls and finely crafted vineyards (with dried-heather thatches to protect the grapes from southwest winds). Smell the rosemary. Study the structure of the town, and pick out the scant remains of an old fort. Notice the S-shape of the main road—once a riverbed—that flows through town. The town's roofs are traditionally made of locally quarried slate and held down by rocks during windstorms.

Halfway along the lip of the ravine, a path marked *Panoramico Volastra (Corniglia)* leads steeply up into the vineyards on the right. This path passes a variety of simple wooden religious scenes, the work of local resident Mario Andreoli. Before his father died, Mario promised him he'd replace the old cross on the family's vineyard. Mario has been adding figures ever since. On religious holidays, everything's lit up: the Nativity, the Last Supper, the Crucifixion, the Resurrection, and more. Some of the scenes are left up year-round. (You can see more of his figures across the ravine, in a little open patch between buildings.)

High above, a recent fire burned off the tree cover, revealing ancient terraces that line the terrain like a topographic map. This path also marks the start of the scenic route to Volastra, on the hilltop above, and eventually to Corniglia (this challenging route is described on page 30).

▸ *Continue on the level trail around the base of the hill. Soon the harbor comes into view. Keep looping around the hill for even better views of town. Once you're facing the sea (after passing the cemetery peninsula below you), the trail takes a sharp left and heads down toward the water on concrete steps. Once on the lower path, continue back across the vineyards toward the harbor. When you're almost back to town, you'll see the entrance (on your right) to...*

The Cemetery

Ever since Napoleon—who was king of Italy in the early 1800s—decreed that cemeteries were health risks, Cinque Terre's burial spots have been located outside the towns. The result: The dearly departed generally get first-class sea views. Each cemetery—with evocative yellowed photos and finely carved Carrara marble memorial reliefs—is worth a visit (Manarola's is the most easily accessible).

Manarola's cemetery and trail overlook the Mediterranean.

In cemeteries like these, there's a hierarchy of four places to park your mortal remains: a graveyard, a spacious death condo *(loculo),* a mini bone-niche *(ossario),* or the communal ossuary. Because of the tight space, a time limit is assigned to the first three options (although many older tombs are grandfathered in). Bones go into the ossuary in the middle of the chapel floor after about a generation. Traditionally, locals make weekly visits to loved ones here, often bringing flowers. The rolling stepladder makes access to top-floor *loculi* easy.

▶ *The Manarola cemetery is on...*

Punta Bonfiglio

This point offers some of the most commanding views of the entire region. To find the best vantage point, take the stairs just below the cemetery (through the green gate), then walk farther out toward the water through a park (playground, drinking water, WC, and picnic benches). Your Manarola finale is the bench at the tip of the point. Pause and take in the view. The easiest way back to town is to take the stairs at the end of the point, which join the main walking path—offering spectacular town views on the way back to the harbor, where we started.

EXPERIENCES IN MANAROLA

Hikes from Manarola

From Manarola, the coastal trail leads to **Corniglia** in one direction, and to **Riomaggiore** (on the easy and romantic Via dell'Amore) in the other. But in recent years both trails have been closed at times due to landslides; check the latest before you head out. If—as is often the case—the main Corniglia trail is closed, consider taking the **high route to Corniglia via Volastra** (much easier if you ride the shuttle bus, rather than hike, up to Volastra). For details, see "Hiking the Cinque Terre" on page 23.

One of my favorite easy hikes in the region is to head up into the **vineyards above Manarola,** then drop down into the town cemetery, enjoying great views on the way. This route is outlined in my self-guided "Manarola Walk."

Hiking Gear and Tips: Cinque Terre Trekking, near the top of the main street (halfway up to the church), is a wonderful resource for hikers. Christine and Nicola are generous with hiking advice, and fill their cramped little shop with all the hiking gear you may need: boots, clothes, walking sticks, maps, and more. If you're serious about hiking, stop in here to confirm your plans and to gear up (daily 9:00-13:00 & 14:00-20:00, shorter hours off-season, Via Discovolo 136, tel. 0187-920-715, www.cinqueterretrekking.com).

Tours

Arbaspàa arranges vineyard wine tastings, cooking classes (6-person minimum), fishing trips, paragliding, rock climbing, and more (see website for options and book in advance, www.arbaspaa.com; their Explora office in Manarola is at Via Discovolo 204, tel. 0187-920-783).

Boat Rides

To get to the dock and the boats that connect Manarola with the other Cinque Terre towns, find the steps to the left of the harbor view—they lead down to the ticket kiosk. Continue around the left side of the cliff (as you're facing the water) to catch the boats.

SLEEPING IN MANAROLA

Manarola has some of the most appealing, well-run accommodations in the region (rivaling Monterosso's). Like the others, it also has plenty of private rooms; ask in bars and restaurants. If you need breakfast, the recommended Café Aristide is your best choice. Otherwise grab a coffee and croissant in a bar.

To transfer luggage from the station to your accommodations, call ahead and arrange with Roberto, based in Monterosso (€15 for all your bags, mobile 329-896-6219).

In the Residential Zone Above the Church

This area is a 10-minute steeply uphill hike from the train station—just huff up the main drag to the church. All of these are within a five-minute walk from there.

$$$$ La Torretta offers 12 trendy, upscale rooms (most with private deck) that cater to a demanding clientele. Probably the most elegant retreat in the region, this peaceful refuge has all the comforts for those happy to pay, including a communal hot tub with a view. Guests enjoy a complimentary snack and glass of prosecco on arrival, wine tastings, an ample breakfast buffet, and minibars. Each chic room is distinct (top-end family suite, book several months in advance, closed Dec-March; on request, they'll pick you up at the station tunnel in a golf cart; on Piazza della Chiesa beside the bell tower at Vico Volto 20, tel. 0187-920-327, www.torrettas.com, torretta@cdh.it).

$$ B&B Da Baranin, with seven good rooms and three apartments, is a bit too pricey but has sleek modern style (family rooms, air-con, Via Aldo Rollandi 29, tel. 0187-920-595, www.baranin.com, info@baranin.com, Sara).

$ Aria di Mare Rooms rents four sunny, tidy, well-equipped rooms and an apartment a few steps beyond Trattoria dal Billy at the very top of town. While it's a steep hike up (high above the tourists), this is an excellent value. Three rooms have spacious terraces with knockout views and lounge chairs (RS%, includes breakfast snacks in room, air-con, upstairs on the left at Via Aldo Rollandi 137, mobile 349-058-4155, www.ariadimare.info, info@ariadimare.info, Maurizio, ask at Billy's if no one's home).

¢ Ostello 5-Terre, Manarola's modern hostel, occupies the former parochial school above the church square and offers 48 beds and a huge roof terrace. This is not a party hostel—it's a calm place where tranquility is greatly appreciated. They rent dorm rooms as doubles with separated beds. Reserve well in advance (not co-ed except for couples and families, all ages, breakfast extra, office closed 13:00-16:00—except maybe in summer, check-in until 20:00, Via B. Riccobaldi 21, tel. 0187-920-039, mobile 346-532-8078, www.hostel5terre.com, ostello5terre@gmail.com).

On the Main Street

These options line up along the main street, between the harbor and the church. While in a less atmospheric area than the ones near the church, they're closer to the station—and therefore a bit handier for those packing heavy.

$$$ Albergo Ca' d'Andrean is quiet, comfortable, and chic. It has 10 big, sunny, industrial-mod rooms, with lots of tile and concrete. Public spaces artfully display family artifacts, and the cool garden oasis comes complete with lemon trees. If you don't mind stairs, consider one of their pricier top-floor rooms, with great views from their terraces (breakfast extra, air-con, up the hill at Via Discovolo 101, tel. 0187-920-040, www.cadandrean.it, info@cadandrean.it, Simone and Nicola).

$$$ Marina Piccola, a lesser value, offers 12 stylish rooms on the water (some with sea views). It's expensive and impersonal, but it's handy to the harbor area (air-con, Via Birolli 120, tel. 0187-920-770, www.hotelmarinapiccola.com, info@hotelmarinapiccola.com).

$$ At Da Paulin, charming Donatella and Eraldo (the town's retired policeman) rent three surprisingly modern, fresh, well-equipped, air-conditioned, hotelesque rooms with a large and inviting common living room. They also rent three apartments (fans). This fine value is at the bend in the main street, a five-minute hike above the train tracks (no breakfast, Via Discovolo 126, mobile 334-389-4764, www.dapaulin.it, prenotazioni@dapaulin.it).

High Above Manarola, in Volastra

$$ Hotel il Saraceno, with seven spacious, modern rooms, is a deal for drivers. Located above Manarola in the tiny town of Volastra (chock-full of vacationing Germans and Italians in summer), it's serene, clean, and right by the shuttle bus to Manarola (free parking, tel. 0187-760-081, www.thesaraceno.com, hotel@thesaraceno.com, friendly Antonella).

EATING IN MANAROLA

Restaurant options are limited in Manarola, but you have at least two excellent options: Billy's and Aristide. I've listed the options from lowest to highest, in terms of both quality and elevation.

The vast majority of the town's (decidedly touristy) restaurants are concentrated between Piazza Capellini and the harbor. They are mostly interchangeable, but the Scorza family works hard at **$$ Trattoria il Porticciolo** (Thu-Tue 12:00-21:30, closed Wed, Via Birolli 92, tel. 0187-920-083). At the harborfront, **$$$ Marina Piccola** is famous for great views, lousy service, and overcharging naive tourists (closed Mon).

$$ Ristorante di Aristide, right on Piazza Capellini, is run by three generations of hardworking women and offers a trendy atmosphere and a pleasant outdoor setting, with a view of budding soccer stars rather than harborfront glitz (Fri-Wed 12:00-22:30). Down the stairs, at the bottom of the main street, their **$ café** has indoor and streetside seating, a simpler menu, and breakfast options (omelets, pizzas, sandwiches, salads; open

Fri-Wed from 8:00, food served until restaurant opens for dinner; both closed Thu and Jan-Feb, Via Discovolo 290, tel. 0187-920-000, charming Elena, Mamma Monica, and Nonna Grazia).

Via Discovolo, the main street climbing up through town from Piazza Capellini to the church, is lined with simpler places, including a popular *gelateria* and some small grocery stores where you can browse for a picnic. This strip—and the short street between the elevated square and the harbor—also has several focaccia, pizza-by-the-slice, and fried-goodies carryout shops that are fine for a quick lunch.

Up at the residential zone above the church, dining options are sparse, but the place that's here is a good one: **$$$ Trattoria dal Billy.** Many find it's worth the climb for Edoardo and chef Enrico's homemade black pasta with seafood and squid ink, green pasta with artichokes, and homemade desserts. Their *antipasto misto di mare* comes with a dazzling array of seafood treats—each one perfectly executed. Billy's outdoor terraces offer commanding views over Manarola, while across the street an elegant, glassy dining room is carved into the rock. Either setting is perfect for a romantic candlelight meal. Dinner reservations are a must (Fri-Wed 12:00-15:00 & 18:00-22:00, closed Thu, Via Aldo Rollandi 122, tel. 0187-920-628, www.trattoriabilly.com).

Riomaggiore

The most substantial town of the group, Riomaggiore is a disappointment from the train station. But just walk through the tunnel next to the tracks, and you'll discover a more real and laid-back town than its more touristy neighbors. The main drag, while traffic-free, feels more urban than "village," and surrounding the harbor is a fascinating tangle of pastel homes leaning on each other like drunken sailors. Despite Riomaggiore's workaday soul, the views back on its harbor from the breakwater—especially at sunset—are some of the region's prettiest.

ORIENTATION TO RIOMAGGIORE

Tourist Information

Tourist information is skimpy here. There are two "TIs" at the train station—one is actually the train ticket window, and the other is a shop for the national park (both open daily 8:00-20:00, shorter hours off-season)—but both can be too busy to be helpful. If you're in a pinch for tourist information, try asking Amy and Francesco at Riomaggiore Reservations (see "Sleeping in Riomaggiore," later) or Ivo and Alberto at the recommended Bar Centrale.

Arrival in Riomaggiore

By Train: Riomaggiore's train station is separated from the town center by a steep hill. To get to the center, take the pedestrian tunnel that begins by the big mural (and parallels the rail tunnel). You'll exit at the bottom of Via Colombo; most recommended accommodations are a short hike up this steep artery.

If you're staying near the top of town, you can catch the sporadic shuttle bus at the bottom of Via Colombo and ride it partway up, or pay €1 to ride the elevator up from the pedestrian tunnel (if it's running—often closed for repairs). For a scenic route into town (for those not carrying luggage), take my "Riomaggiore Walk," later.

By Car: Day-trippers park at one of two pay-and-display lots above town (€3.50/hour, €23/day). If you're staying overnight, your hotel may have parking. Otherwise, Riomaggiore allows overnighters to drive into the town center long enough to drop off or pick up bags, but only during designated times (confirm with your hotelier). It may be easier to park at La Spezia's train station and ride the train in.

Workaday Riomaggiore feels lived in, where every day is laundry day.

Helpful Hints

Baggage Storage and Delivery: You can check your bag at the casually run ***deposito bagagli* office,** which is straight ahead as you exit the station (€3/bag, daily 8:30-19:00, closed in winter). If you want help hauling your bags to your hotel, **Roberto** will do it for €5 per bag. He can also deliver your bags to other towns so they're waiting for you at the other end of a hike (call ahead to arrange, mobile 329-896-6219).

Services: A WC is near the Co-op grocery on Via Colombo, and another is under the tunnel where the street dead-ends.

Laundry: A self-service launderette is on the main street (daily in summer 8:30-20:00, shorter hours off-season, Via Colombo 107).

RIOMAGGIORE WALK

Here's a partly uphill but easy self-guided loop walk that takes the long way around from the station into town. You'll enjoy some fine views before strolling down the main street to the harbor.

▸ *Start at the train station. (If you arrive by boat, cross beneath the tracks and take a left, then hike through the tunnel along the tracks to reach the station.) You'll see some...*

Murals brighten the approach to Riomaggiore.

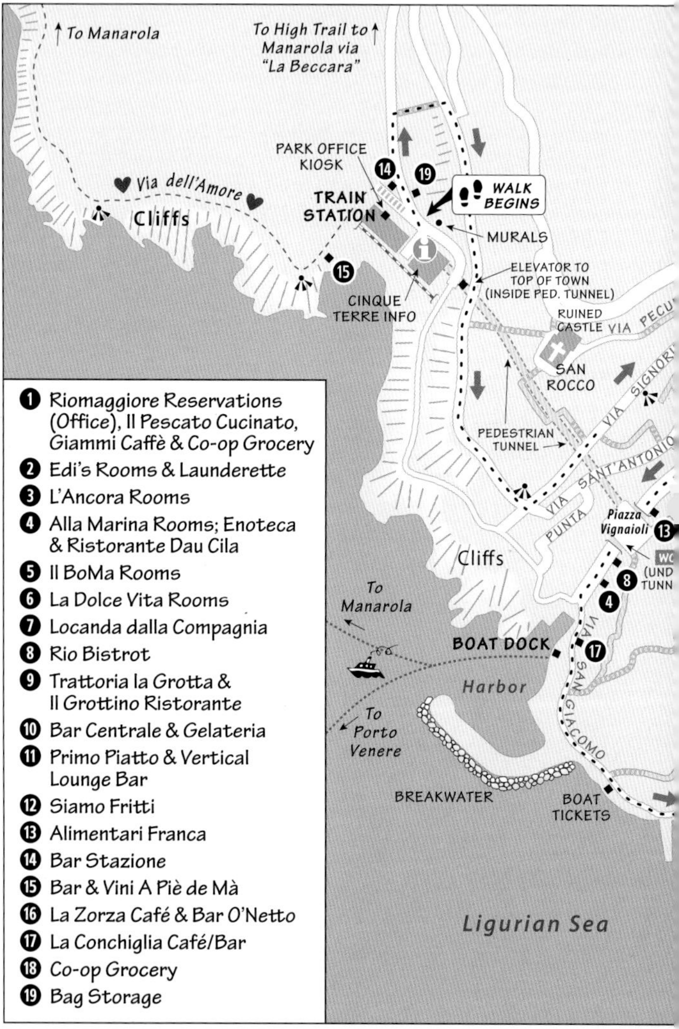
To Manarola
To High Trail to Manarola via "La Beccara"
PARK OFFICE KIOSK
TRAIN STATION
WALK BEGINS
MURALS
Via dell'Amore
Cliffs
ELEVATOR TO TOP OF TOWN (INSIDE PED. TUNNEL)
CINQUE TERRE INFO
RUINED CASTLE
VIA PECU
SAN ROCCO
VIA SIGNORI
PEDESTRIAN TUNNEL
VIA SANT'ANTONIO
VIA PUNTA
Piazza Vignaioli
Cliffs
To Manarola
BOAT DOCK
VIA SAN GIACOMO
Harbor
To Porto Venere
BREAKWATER
BOAT TICKETS
Ligurian Sea
1 Riomaggiore Reservations (Office), Il Pescato Cucinato, Giammi Caffè & Co-op Grocery
2 Edi's Rooms & Launderette
3 L'Ancora Rooms
4 Alla Marina Rooms; Enoteca & Ristorante Dau Cila
5 Il BoMa Rooms
6 La Dolce Vita Rooms
7 Locanda dalla Compagnia
8 Rio Bistrot
9 Trattoria la Grotta & Il Grottino Ristorante
10 Bar Centrale & Gelateria
11 Primo Piatto & Vertical Lounge Bar
12 Siamo Fritti
13 Alimentari Franca
14 Bar Stazione
15 Bar & Vini A Piè de Mà
16 La Zorza Café & Bar O'Netto
17 La Conchiglia Café/Bar
18 Co-op Grocery
19 Bag Storage

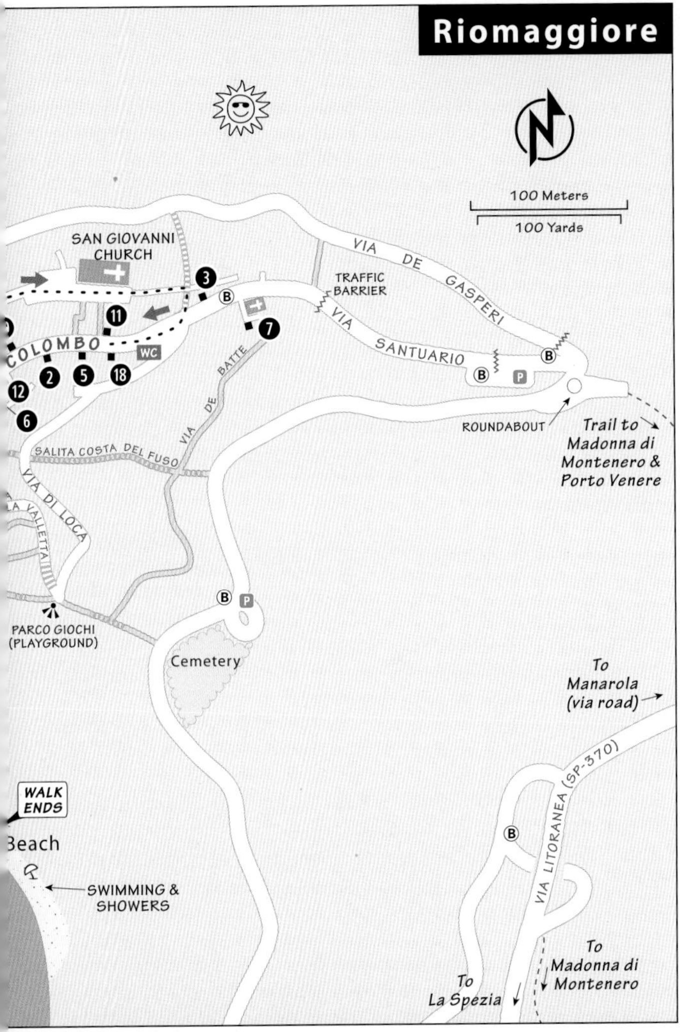
Riomaggiore
100 Meters
100 Yards
SAN GIOVANNI CHURCH
TRAFFIC BARRIER
VIA DE GASPERI
VIA SANTUARIO
COLOMBO
WC
VIA DE BATTE
SALITA COSTA DEL FUSO
VIA DI LOCA
LA VALLETTA
ROUNDABOUT
Trail to Madonna di Montenero & Porto Venere
PARCO GIOCHI (PLAYGROUND)
Cemetery
To Manarola (via road)
VIA LITORANEA (SP-370)
WALK ENDS
Beach
SWIMMING & SHOWERS
To Madonna di Montenero
To La Spezia

Faded Murals

These beautiful murals, with subjects modeled after real-life Riomaggiorians, glorify the nameless workers who constructed the nearly 300 million cubic feet of mortarless, dry-stone walls that run throughout the Cinque Terre. These walls give the region its characteristic *muri a secco* terracing for vineyards and olive groves. Unfortunately, the murals, created by Argentinean artist Silvio Benedetto, were painted on wood panels—and are starting to chip away.

Looking left, notice the stairs climbing up just past the station building. These lead to the easy trail to Manarola, the **Via dell'Amore** (which may be closed for repairs).

▸ *Facing the mural, turn left, then go right up the wide street just before the station café. Head up this street for about 100 yards, and watch for the stairs leading through the garden on your right to the upper switchback. Then, once on high ground, turn right (back toward the sea). Soon you'll pass the top of the concrete elevator tower and, a bit farther, arrive at a fine viewpoint.*

Top o' the Town

Here you're treated to spectacular sea views. When you're ready to move on, hook left around the bluff; rounding the bend, ignore the steps marked *marina seacoast* (which lead to the harbor) and continue another five minutes along level ground to the church, following *salita castello* signs. You'll go by the city hall, with murals celebrating the heroic grape-pickers and fishermen of the region (also by Silvio Benedetto), then pass the town preschool.

▸ *Before reaching the church, pause at the big terrace to enjoy the...*

Town View

The major river of this region once ran through this valley, as implied by the name Riomaggiore (local dialect for "river" and "major"). As in the other Cinque Terre towns, the main street covers its *rio maggiore,* which carved the canyon now filled by the town's pastel high-rises. The romantic arched bridges that once connected the two sides have been replaced by a practical modern road.

Notice the lack of ugly aerial antennae. In the 1980s, every residence got cable. Now, the TV tower on the hilltop behind the church steeple brings the modern world into each home. The church was rebuilt in 1870, but was

Riomaggiore's beach scene is busy by day and romantic by night.

first established in 1340. It's dedicated to St. John the Baptist, the patron saint of Genoa, the maritime republic that once dominated the region.

▶ *Continue straight past the church and along the narrow lane, watching on the right for wide stairs leading down to Riomaggiore's main street...*

Via Colombo

Start downhill. First you'll pass (on the right, at #62) a handy pizzeria/ *focacceria,* facing the Co-op grocery store across the street (at #55). Below that is a delicious fresh pasta takeaway place (Primo Piatto, at #72—handy for a picnic lunch or dinner). Farther along, the big covered terrace on the right belongs to the recommended Bar Centrale, the town's most popular hangout for international visitors (at #144).

As you round the bend to the left, notice the old-timey pharmacy just above (on the right). On your left, at #199, peek into the Il Pescato Cucinato shop, where Laura fries up her husband Edoardo's fresh catch; grab a paper cone of deep-fried seafood as a snack. Where the road bends sharply right, notice the bench on your left (just before La Zorza Café)—the hangout for the town's old-timers, who keep a running commentary on the steady flow of people. Straight ahead, you can already see where this street will dead-end. The last shop on the left, Alimentari Franca (at #251), is a well-stocked grocery where you can gather the makings for a perfect picnic out on the harbor or along the Via dell'Amore.

Where Via Colombo dead-ends, look right to see the tunnel leading back to the station (and the Via dell'Amore to Manarola, and eventually to the other Cinque Terre towns). Look left to see two sets of stairs. The "up" stairs take you to a park-like square built over the train tracks, which provides the children of the town a bit of level land on which to kick their soccer balls. The murals above, marking the town's middle school, celebrate the great-grandparents of these very children—the salt-of-the-earth locals who earned a humble living before the age of tourism. Riomaggiorians are proud that they are the only Cinque Terre town with their own middle school—in the other towns, kids are sent away to school much earlier.

▶ *The "down" stairs take you to a pay WC and the...*

Marina

This most picturesque corner of Riomaggiore features a tight cluster of buildings huddling nervously around a postage-stamp square and vest-pocket harbor. Because Riomaggiore lacks the naturally protected harbor of Vernazza, when bad weather is expected, fishermen pull their boats up to the safety of the little square. This is quite an operation, so it's a team effort—the signal goes out, and anyone with a boat of their own helps move the whole fleet. Sometimes the fishermen are busy beaching their boats even on a bright, sunny day—an indication that they know something you don't.

A couple of recommended restaurants—with high prices and memorable seating—look down over the action. Head past them and up the walkway along the left side of the harbor, and enjoy the views of the town's colorful pastel buildings, with the craggy coastline of the Cinque Terre just beyond. The best views are from up top, in front of the café. Below you, the breakwater curves out to sea, providing a bit of protection for the harbor. These rocks are popular with sunbathers by day and romantics and photographers at sunset.

For a peek at Riomaggiore's beach, continue around the bluff on this trail toward Punta di Montenero, the cape that defines the southern end of the Cinque Terre. As you walk, you'll pass the rugged boat landing and eventually run into Riomaggiore's uncomfortably rocky but still inviting beach *(spiaggia)*. Ponder how Europeans manage to look relaxed when lounging on football-sized "pebbles."

EXPERIENCES IN RIOMAGGIORE

Hikes from Riomaggiore

For an **easy walk** along the lip of the one-time river ravine, take Via di Loca, which veers off the main drag at the top of town (directly across from the stairs at the upper end of Via Colombo—described earlier, in my self-guided

walk). This leads in just a few minutes to the town playground *(parco giochi),* benches, neighborhood pea patches, and pleasant views over town (especially at sunset). There's also a steep staircase from here up to the town cemetery; from there, an even steeper trail runs all the way up to the town's sanctuary (though there's an easier alternative—described next).

For a **scenic one-hour trail** that rises from Riomaggiore to the 14th-century **Madonna di Montenero sanctuary,** high above the town, take the main road inland until you see signs at the roundabout at the top of town; or ride the shuttle bus 12 minutes from the town center to the sanctuary trail, then walk uphill another 15 minutes (great picnic spot up top).

For other hikes from Riomaggiore—the Via dell'Amore trail to Manarola, the steep 1.5-hour "La Beccara" hike over the bluff to Manarola, and the five-hour trail to Porto Venere, see page 28.

Beach

Riomaggiore's rugged and tiny "beach" is rocky, but it's clean and peaceful.

It's just around the bluff from the harbor, past the boat landing—to find it, see the end of my self-guided walk, above. There's a shower here in the summer, and another closer to town by the boat landing—where many enjoy sunning on and jumping from the rocks.

Kayaks and Water Sports

Diving Center 5 Terre has kayaks, snorkeling, scuba classes, and more (daily May-Sept 9:00-18:00, open only in good weather, likely weekends only in shoulder season, office down the stairs and under the tracks on Via San Giacomo, tel. 0187-920-011, www.5terrediving.it).

NIGHTLIFE IN RIOMAGGIORE

With a youthful spirit and lively evening bustle, Riomaggiore may have the Cinque Terre's most appealing nightlife. Stroll the main drag, scope out these listings (serving €6-8 cocktails), and find the one that appeals. Several of these places have full menus if you want to eat.

Bar Centrale, run by sociable Ivo, Alberto, and the gang, offers "nightlife" any time of day—it's a magnet for tourists (and a few young locals, too). Ivo, who lived in the Bay Area, fills his bar with San Franciscan rock and a fun-loving vibe; it feels a little like the village's living room (great mojitos, daily 7:30-late, free Wi-Fi with drink, Via Colombo 144).

Enoteca & Ristorante Dau Cila is a mellow little hideaway with a jazz-and-Brazilian-lounge ambience. Located down at the minuscule harbor, it's cool for cocktails and open nightly until midnight (snacks and meals, fine wine by the glass, Via San Giacomo 65).

Bar & Vini A Piè de Mà, at the Via dell'Amore trailhead, has piles of charm, frequent music, and stays open until midnight June through September.

More Bars and Cafés: Near the bottom of Via Colombo, facing each other, are the hip **La Zorza Café** (appealing to international tourists with thumping music and freestyle bartender) and the classier **Bar O'Netto** (geared more for locals, with a mellower vibe and nice outdoor seating). Higher up on Via Colombo (at #76), **Vertical Lounge Bar** has a lively and loose ambience, light food, and a fine people-watching perch near the top of the promenade zone. And at sunset, you can't beat **La**

Conchiglia—the simple café/bar on the bluff overlooking the harbor—a perfect location for watching the sun disappear into the Ligurian Sea and the lights of Monterosso twinkling on the horizon.

Twilight Hike: The marvelous (currently closed) **Via dell'Amore** trail, lit only with subtle ground lighting so that you can see the stars, welcomes romantics after dark. When open, the trail is free after the ticket booth closes (typically around 19:00).

SLEEPING IN RIOMAGGIORE

Given the relatively lousy value of most Riomaggiore hotels, I recommend staying in one of the town's many private rooms for rent. Very few private rooms include breakfast; for ideas, see "Breakfast," later.

Room-Booking Services

Several room-booking agencies—with relatively predictable office hours, English-speaking staff, and email addresses—line up within a few yards of each other on Via Colombo. Each manages a corral of local rooms for rent; the quality and specific amenities can vary wildly, so get a complete picture of the room before you commit. These offices sometimes close unexpectedly, so it's smart to settle up the day before you leave in case they're closed when you need to depart. Expect lots of stairs—ask how many when you book.

$ Riomaggiore Reservations, run with care by American expat Amy and her Italian husband, Francesco, offers six rooms and six apartments (RS%, cash only, reception open daily 9:00-13:00 & 14:00-17:00 in season, some rooms have air-con, Via Colombo 181, tel. 0187-760-575, www.riomaggiorereservations.com, info@riomaggiorereservations.com).

$ Edi's Rooms manages four double rooms and twelve apartments. You pay extra for views (family rooms, office open daily in summer 8:30-20:00, in winter 10:30-12:30 & 14:30-18:00, some rooms with air-con, closed Jan-Feb, reception at Via Colombo 111, tel. 0187-760-842, www.appartamenticinqueterre.net, edi-vesigna@iol.it). They also rent three hotelesque but pricey rooms of their own, called **$$ L'Ancora** (air-con, no breakfast, www.lancoracinqueterre.com).

Rooms for Rent *(Affittacamere)*

Another option is to book directly with someone who rents just a few rooms of their own.

$$ Alla Marina is Riomaggiore's best value, with five rooms and an apartment at the top of one of the very tall, skinny buildings that rise up from the harbor. The furnishings are a stylish combination of modern and nautical, and friendly brothers Sandro and Andrea take pride in running a tight ship (RS%, one cheaper nonview room, breakfast served in-room, snacks, air-con, free minibar, pay parking, Via San Giacomo 61—ask about the easier back-door entrance, mobile 328-013-4077, www.allamarina.com, info@allamarina.com). They also rent several rooms in other parts of town.

$$ Il BoMa—named for the owners, American Maddy and her Italian husband, Bombetta—has three pricey but well-appointed rooms right along the main drag. They also rent three nearby apartments (includes in-room breakfast with freshly baked brioche, one cheaper room has private bathroom down the hall and fans, others have air-con, up three flights at Via Colombo 99, tel. 0187-920-395, mobile 320-0748826, www.ilboma.com, info@ilboma.it).

$ La Dolce Vita offers six modern, good-value rooms on the main drag, plus two apartments elsewhere in town (some with air-con, no breakfast, open daily 9:30-19:30—if they're closed, they're full; Via Colombo 167, tel. 0187-762-283, agonatal@libero.it, helpful Giacomo and Simone).

$ Locanda dalla Compagnia, loosely run by Alessandro, rents five rooms at the top of town, just 300 yards below the parking lot and tucked behind a little church. All rooms—decent but rather dim and dated—are on the same tranquil ground floor and share a lounge (air-con, mini-fridge, no views, reception closes at 19:00, Via del Santuario 239, tel. 0187-760-050, www.dallacompa.com, lacomp@libero.it).

EATING IN RIOMAGGIORE

For more options, see "Nightlife in Riomaggiore," earlier.

On the Harbor

Harborfront dining comes with slightly higher prices but glorious views. These two eateries share the same owner; the first one's menu is more traditionally Italian, while the second is a bit more modern.

$$$$ Enoteca & Ristorante Dau Cila (pronounced "dow CHEE-lah") is decked out like a black-and-white movie set in a centuries-old boat shed with extra tables outside on a rustic deck over dinghies. Try their antipasto specialty of several seafood appetizers and listen to the waves lapping at the harbor below (cheaper lunch menu with salads and *bruschette,* daily 12:00-24:00, closed Feb, Via San Giacomo 65, tel. 0187-760-032, Luca).

$$$$ Rio Bistrot, small and intimate at the top of the harbor, tries to jazz up its Ligurian cuisine with international influences. You can order à la carte from the short but well-designed menu, but they tend to push their €37 tasting menu (simpler and cheaper lunch menu, daily 12:00-16:00 & 18:00-22:00, Via San Giacomo 46, tel. 0187-920-616).

On the Main Street, Via Colombo

$$ Trattoria la Grotta, right in the town center (with no view), has a passion for anchovies and mussels. You'll enjoy reliably good food and friendly service surrounded by historical photos and wonderful stonework in a dramatic, dressy, cave-like setting. Vanessa is warm and helpful, while her mother, Isa, is busy cooking (daily 12:00-14:30 & 17:30-22:30, closed Wed in winter, Via Colombo 247, tel. 0187-920-187). Next door and run by the same family, **$$$ Il Grottino Ristorante** is slightly more upscale (same hours but closed Wed in winter, tel. 0187-920-938).

$$ Bar Centrale, the popular bar and expat hangout listed earlier under "Nightlife in Riomaggiore," has a menu of Italian specialties (pasta dishes, anchovies) and a few American comfort food standbys like hamburgers. They also have a *gelateria* on site (open long hours daily).

Light Meals: Various handy carry-out eateries along the main drag offer good lunches or snacks. Choose a bench on Via Colombo, or head out to the breakwater for a scenic munch. **$ Primo Piatto,** at the top of town, offers takeaway handmade pastas and sauces, cooked to order on the spot. It's cheap and delicious (Wed-Mon 10:30-19:30 or later, closed Tue, Via Colombo 72, tel. 0187-920-038). For deep-fried seafood in a paper cone, I like **$ Il Pescato Cucinato,** where Edoardo fishes and his wife, Laura, fries (chalkboard out front explains what's fresh, daily 11:20-20:30, near the bottom of Via Colombo at #199, mobile 339-262-4815). A few doors away, **$ Siamo Fritti** also has fried fish (daily 10:00-21:00, Via Colombo 161, mobile 347-826-1729, Andrea and Isabella).

Picnics: Groceries and delis lining Via Colombo sell food to go for a picnic at the harbor or beach. The two **Co-op** grocery stores have the best prices. For a more appetizing selection and good service, head to the handy **Alimentari Franca,** at the very bottom of the main street, right by the train-station tunnel and stairs to the marina/beach (daily 8:00-12:45 & 15:30-19:30, Via Colombo 251).

Breakfast: For eggs or a good croissant-and-espresso fix, drop by **Bar Centrale** (described earlier); **Giammi Caffè,** with outdoor tables on the main drag (daily 7:00-24:00, Via Colombo 189, mobile 331-608-3512); or **Bar Stazione,** at the train station.

Near the Train Station and Via dell'Amore

$$ Bar & Vini A Piè de Mà, at the trailhead on the Manarola end of town, is good for a scenic light bite or quiet drink at night. The downstairs bar, with great outdoor seating, is self-service: Head into the bar to place your order, then bring it out to your preferred perch (daily 10:00-20:00, June-Sept until 24:00, closed Mon-Tue off-season, free Wi-Fi, tel. 0187-921-037). Enjoy a meal on its dramatically situated terrace for an indelible Cinque Terre memory. In the summer they open a restaurant with table service upstairs—but I prefer the cheaper, simpler terrace.

Enjoy a coffee from your perch above the sea near the station.

Near the Cinque Terre

The Cinque Terre is tops, but there's much more to the Italian Riviera. To the north of the Cinque Terre is a trio of beach towns: Levanto, the northern gateway to the Cinque Terre; Sestri Levante, stunningly situated on a narrow peninsula flanked by two beaches; and Santa Margherita Ligure, a thriving city with an active waterfront and easy connections to yacht-happy Portofino. At the other end of the Cinque Terre is the pretty resort of Porto Venere (pictured above) and the region's gritty transit hub, La Spezia.

After exploring the villages and trails of the Cinque Terre, visiting these Riviera towns feels like a return to civilization—for reasons both good and bad (modern amenities, urban scene, and traffic).

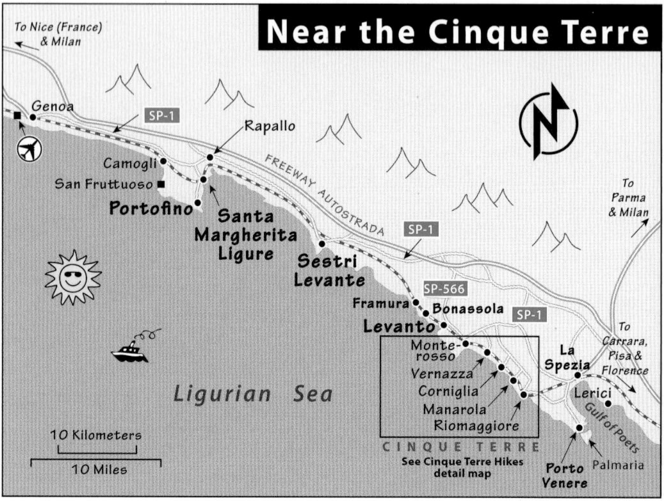

Home Bases: Levanto, Sestri Levante, and Santa Margherita Ligure are practical home bases for drivers wanting to park at their hotel and side-trip to the Cinque Terre by train, or for those who want modern hotels with all the predictable resort amenities. (They're also worth a look if you're finding the Cinque Terre towns booked up.)

Levanto—just minutes beyond Monterosso by train—is the handiest. Sestri Levante is a bit farther away with a little less train service. Santa Margherita Ligure is the most distant and requires a transfer on most connections to the Cinque Terre, but the town compensates by being the most appealing—and it gives you easy access to posh Portofino. La Spezia is too plain for a home base, and Porto Venere works best as a day trip.

If you home-base near the Cinque Terre, keep in mind that you'll be competing with other day-trippers for space on prime midday trains to and from the Cinque Terre. Turn this problem into an advantage: On especially busy days, enjoy your home-base town during the day, then head into the Cinque Terre villages in the late afternoon for untrampled charm, a romantic dinner, and a late train back.

North of the Cinque Terre

When most people imagine the "Italian Riviera," they're thinking of the shimmering resort towns north of the Cinque Terre. Big, stately, Old World hotels loom over crowded pebble beaches with rentable umbrellas. Fastidiously landscaped parks and promenades are jammed with more Italian visitors than American tourists. These towns are perfect for day-tripping—or even an overnight.

Levanto

Graced with a long, sandy beach, Levanto (LEH-vahn-toh) is packed in summer and popular with surfers. The rest of the year, it's just a small, sleepy town. It has a fraction of the charm of the Cinque Terre, but it enjoys fewer crowds, more varied dining options, and quick connections to the Cinque Terre (4 minutes to Monterosso by train, continuing to the rest of the Cinque Terre villages on the same line).

This beach town isn't the "real" Cinque Terre, but it can be a perfectly workable home base (with a high number of family rooms and large, affordable apartments with kitchenettes). From Levanto, you can hop a train or boat to the Cinque Terre towns and beyond; take the no-wimps-allowed hike to Monterosso (3 hours); or bike or stroll on a delightful, level path to the nearby, uncrowded beach town of Bonassola.

Orientation to Levanto

Levanto (pop. 5,600) is dominated by an uninspiring new town, a regular grid street plan of five-story apartment buildings that stretches from the train station down to the broad, curving beach. The sleepy, twisty old town—bisected by a modern street—is tucked up against the adjacent hill.

Tourist Information

A Cinque Terre National Park info center is at the train station. The helpful TI is on Piazza Cavour (daily 9:00-13:00 & 15:00-18:00 except closed Sun afternoon, shorter hours off-season, tel. 0187-808-125, www.comune.levanto.sp.it).

Levanto's harbor is bordered by an elevated promenade.

Arrival in Levanto

By Train: From the train station (no baggage storage), head through the parking lot and down the stairs, turn right, and cross the bridge onto Corso Roma—the main drag. The beach is straight ahead, and most of my recommended hotels, restaurants, and the TI are in the grid of streets to your left. You can walk from the station to most of my recommended places in about 10 minutes.

By Car: If your hotel doesn't offer parking—or if you're not sleeping here—you have three good alternatives. The lots surrounding the **train station** are affordable and handy for hopping a train to the Cinque Terre towns (€1.20/hour, €10.80/day). For longer stays, park in the **free lot** a few blocks north of the station (across the river from the hospital on the way into town—first left after the hospital, cross the bridge and immediately turn left). If you're heading for the beach, the parking lot there is handy but expensive (€1.80/hour, €18/day).

Helpful Hints

Markets: Levanto's modern covered ***mercato,*** which sells produce and fish, is on Via del Mercato, between the train station and the beach (Mon-Sat 8:00-13:00, closed Sun). On Wednesday morning, an **open-air market** with clothes, shoes, and housewares fills the street in front of the *mercato.*

Laundry: A **self-service launderette** stuffed with snack and drink vending machines is at Piazza Staglieno 38, facing an inviting park (open 24 hours daily, mobile 338-701-6341). Another self-service place, **Speedy Wash,** is at Via Garibaldi 32 (daily 8:00-22:00, mobile 338-701-6341).

Bike Rental: Relatively flat Levanto, with light traffic, is a great bike town—and the ride to nearby Bonassola is easy and delightful. Try **Cicli Raso North Shore** (€10-20/day depending on type of bike, daily 9:30-12:30 & 15:30-19:00, closed Sun Nov-April, Via Garibaldi 63, tel. 0187-802-511, www.cicliraso.com), or the **Sensafreni Bike Shop,** which is convenient to the beach boardwalk (€3/hour, €5/half-day, €15/all day, Mon-Sat 9:30-12:30 & 16:00-19:30, closed Sun, Piazza del Popolo 1, tel. 0187-807-128).

Electric Bike Tours: Ebikein offers a variety of guided tours on electric bikes—giving you a helpful boost on the hills. Options range from a 2.5-hour loop around town (€39) to an ambitious 4-hour pedal up to

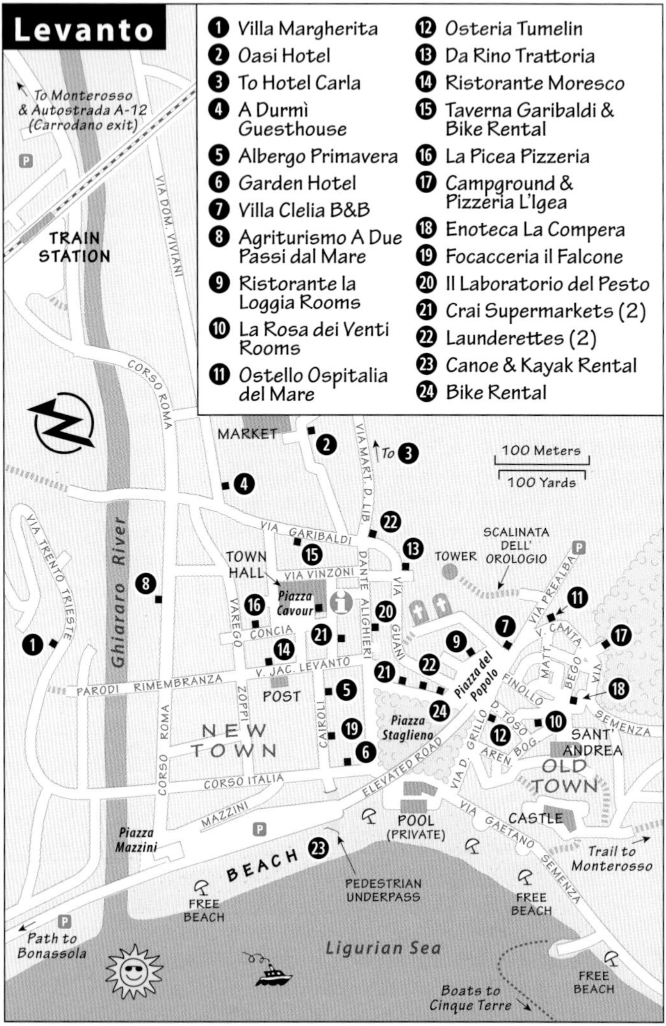
Levanto
1 Villa Margherita
2 Oasi Hotel
3 To Hotel Carla
4 A Durmì Guesthouse
5 Albergo Primavera
6 Garden Hotel
7 Villa Clelia B&B
8 Agriturismo A Due Passi dal Mare
9 Ristorante la Loggia Rooms
10 La Rosa dei Venti Rooms
11 Ostello Ospitalia del Mare
12 Osteria Tumelin
13 Da Rino Trattoria
14 Ristorante Moresco
15 Taverna Garibaldi & Bike Rental
16 La Picea Pizzeria
17 Campground & Pizzeria L'Igea
18 Enoteca La Compera
19 Focacceria il Falcone
20 Il Laboratorio del Pesto
21 Crai Supermarkets (2)
22 Launderettes (2)
23 Canoe & Kayak Rental
24 Bike Rental
To Monterosso & Autostrada A-12 (Carrodano exit)
TRAIN STATION
VIA DOM. VIVIANI
CORSO ROMA
MARKET
VIA MART. D. LIB.
To 3
100 Meters
100 Yards
VIA GARIBALDI
TOWN HALL
VIA VINZONI
Piazza Cavour
TOWER
SCALINATA DELL' OROLOGIO
VIA PREALBA
V. CANTA
VIA TRENTO TRIESTE
Ghiararo River
VAREGO
CONCIA
DANTE ALIGHIERI
VIA GUANI
MATT.
BEGO
VIA
V. JAC. LEVANTO
Piazza del Popolo
FINOLLO
PARODI
RIMEMBRANZA
ZOPPI
POST
D. TOSO
SEMENZA
Piazza Stagliene
NEW TOWN
CAIROLI
GRILLO
AREN.
BOG.
SANT' ANDREA
CORSO ROMA
OLD TOWN
CORSO ITALIA
ELEVATED ROAD
VIA D.
MAZZINI
POOL (PRIVATE)
VIA GAETANO SEMENZA
CASTLE
Piazza Mazzini
BEACH
Trail to Monterosso
PEDESTRIAN UNDERPASS
FREE BEACH
FREE BEACH
Path to Bonassola
Ligurian Sea
FREE BEACH
Boats to Cinque Terre

some of the sanctuaries over Cinque Terre towns (€55, also pricey rentals, www.ebikein.com, mobile 334-190-0496).

Sports Rentals: Rosa dei Venti rents kayaks, canoes, surfboards, and windsurfing equipment right on the beach (Marco's mobile 329-451-1981 or 335-608-9277, www.levantorosadeiventi.it).

Sights in Levanto

Beach

Levanto's beach hides below a parking lot and promenade that's elevated above the sand—look for underpasses or stairs along its length. There are pretty boardwalks up on the elevated promenade and down along the beachfront. As you face the harbor, the boat dock is to your far left, and the diving center is to your far right (rental boats available at either place in summer). You can also rent a kayak or canoe just below the east end of the Piazza Mazzini parking lot.

During the summer, three parts of the beach are free: both sides of the boat dock, and near Piazza Mazzini. The rest of the beach is broken up into private sections that charge admission. You can always stroll along the beach, even through the private sections—just don't sit down. Off-season, roughly October through May, the entire beach is free, and you can lay your towel anywhere you like.

Old Town

The old town clusters around Piazza del Popolo. Until a few decades ago, the town's open-air market was held at the 13th-century loggia (covered set of archways) in the square. Explore the back streets.

Hike to Monterosso

This strenuous, three-hour hike is described in more detail on page 33. To begin in Levanto, start at the old town's Piazza del Popolo, and head uphill to the striped church, Chiesa di Sant'Andrea. From the church courtyard, follow the sign to the *castello* (a private residence), go under the stone arch, and continue uphill. From here, you'll take trail SVA (following signs toward Punta Mesco, the rugged tip of the peninsula), then drop steeply down into Monterosso. (If you have weak knees, consider starting in Monterosso instead.)

Hike or Bike to Bonassola (and Framura)

Tucked just off the main train line on a cove north of Levanto, the small beach resort of Bonassola (boh-nah-SOH-lah, pop. 950) is a peaceful little eddy. As far as Riviera beach resorts go, this is a jewel. With a low-key vibe, a tidy grid street plan that feels almost French, and a picturesque dark-sand beach hemmed in by jagged bluffs, Bonassola is a fine alternative to the region's other beaches. And the next best thing to a beach day in Bonassola is getting there: A level, easy, rails-to-trails path cuts through the mountain from Levanto—enjoyable by foot, but even better by bike.

Getting There: Local **trains** run between Levanto and Bonassola (hourly, 3 minutes—requires a change from the Cinque Terre line). But I'd rather take the **promenade.** At the northern end of Levanto's beachfront road/parking lot, you'll find a level, roughly 1.5-mile path neatly divided into bike and pedestrian lanes. Most of the route is through well-lit former train tunnels, with brief breaks overlooking the sea (and hikes down to secluded beaches). The walk takes about 30 minutes, with long stretches through cool tunnels; by bike, it's less than 10 minutes.

Visiting Bonassola: The town itself—with manicured promenades and piazzas—is worth exploring. **$$ Caffè delle Rose,** facing the town's elevated road (at Via Fratelli Rezzano 22), has good gelato, food, and drinks. Several *foccacerie* and other eateries cluster at the far end of town.

The beach is separated from the town center by the elevated road (shared by bikes, walkers, and a parking lot). The inviting **beach** has mostly private sections, with a few free public areas.

For a scenic **walk/hike,** head to the far (north) end of the beach, where a promenade snakes along the base of the cliff (with rocky perches for sunbathing and swimming). For higher views, find the stairs near the

From Bonassola, a promenade continues to Framura.

Bonassola's beach is encircled by rocky bluffs.

flagpole, and follow the steps up on the right side of the yellow church. Popping out at the top, turn left along the scenic, private road as it curls around the top of the bay, with great views back on the town and beach; the path ends at the blocky little Madonnina della Punta chapel.

Bonassola to Framura (best for bikers): From Bonassola, the promenade continues another 1.5 miles to the town of **Framura**—a settlement made up of five hamlets scattered across a hillside. Because this part of the route is almost entirely through tunnels, it's boring for walkers—but quick for bikers. You'll pop out overlooking Framura's rocky little harbor, behind its train station (no direct access—don't count on taking your bike back on the train). Hike down to the harbor, or up to the village—or simply enjoy the views, then turn around and pedal back to Bonassola and Levanto.

Sleeping in Levanto

$$$ Villa Margherita is across the river and a bit uphill (about a 10-minute walk from the town center or train station), but the shaded gardens, 11 characteristic colorfully tiled rooms, and tranquility are worth the walk (family rooms, air-con, elevator one flight up from street level, free parking, Via Trento e Trieste 31, tel. 0187-807-212, mobile 328-842-6934, www.villamargherita.net, info@villamargherita.net).

$$$ Oasi Hotel, well-run by Silvia, has 14 rooms in a cozy small hotel behind the market hall. Some rooms have balconies, others have direct access to the garden, and a few have neither—request your choice when you reserve (air-con, elevator, parking extra, Via Ferraro, tel. 0187-807-356, www.oasihotel.eu, info@oasihotel.eu).

$$$ Hotel Carla sits in a humdrum residential zone, about 10 minutes from the beach and the station. Its 30 rooms come with surprising style—most have balconies, and all are decorated in soothing, neutral colors (family rooms, air-con, elevator, Via Martiri della Libertà 28, tel. 0187-808-275, www.carlahotel.com, info@carlahotel.com).

$$ A Durmì is a happy little guesthouse owned by lovely Graziella, Gianni, and their two daughters, Elisa and Chiara. Their sunny patios, green leafy gardens, six immaculate beach bungalow-type rooms, and five sunlit apartments make this a welcoming place to stay (breakfast extra, family rooms, air-con, bar, pay parking, Via D. Viviani 12, tel. 0187-800-823, mobile 349-105-6016, www.adurmi.it, info@adurmi.it).

$$ Albergo Primavera is family-run, with 17 colorful rooms—10 with balconies (but no views)—just a half-block from the beach (family rooms, request a quiet room off the street, includes hearty breakfast buffet, air-con, pay parking, free loaner bikes, Via Cairoli 5, tel. 0187-808-023, www.primaverahotel.com, info@primaverahotel.com; friendly Carlo, cheerful Daniela, and daughters Giuditta and Gloria).

$$ Garden Hotel offers 17 functional, modern rooms (all with balconies but no views) on the first floor of an apartment building. While it's a lesser value, you're paying for proximity to the beach—it's just across the street (more expensive fifth-floor rooms have sea views and terrace, closed Nov-mid-March, air-con, elevator for fifth floor only, free parking but not on-site, loaner bikes, Corso Italia 6, tel. 0187-808-173, www.nuovogarden.com, info@nuovogarden.com, Davide and Damiano).

$$ Villa Clelia B&B offers five dark, air-conditioned rooms (named for the winds—*scirocco, maestrale,* and so on) with minifridges and terraces. The rooms, on an exterior corridor, surround a garden courtyard just a short walk up from the sea (minimal in-room breakfast, free parking; with loggia on your left, it's straight ahead at Piazza da Passano 1; tel.

0187-808-195, mobile 329-379-4859, www.villaclelia.it, info@villaclelia.it). Their central apartments economically sleep up to five.

$ Agriturismo A Due Passi dal Mare is an in-town oasis, just a five-minute walk from the beach or the train station. Friendly Francesca and husband Maurizio rent four crisp, quiet rooms—with sizable bathrooms—in the 1920s home built by her grandfather; their back garden is open to guests (free on-site parking, closed Jan-Feb, right on the main drag at Corso Roma 37, tel. 0187-809-177, mobile 338-960-1537, www.a2passidalmare.com, info@a2passidalmare.com).

$ Ristorante la Loggia has eight cozy and older—yet cheap—rooms perched above the old loggia on Piazza del Popolo (cash only, request balcony, quieter rooms in back, two basic side-by-side apartments great for families of 4-8, lots of stairs, air-con, free parking, reception open 9:00-23:00, Piazza del Popolo 7, tel. 0187-808-107, mobile 335-641-7701, www.loggialevanto.com, Nerina does not speak English).

$$ La Rosa dei Venti is an *affittacamere* just a couple of blocks from the beach, in the old town. Enthusiastic Rosanna and her son Marco rent five old-fashioned, overpriced rooms with dark hardwood floors, comfy rugs, and glittery seashore decor (air-con, free parking, across from Piazza del Popolo, Via della Compera, tel. 0187-808-165, Marco's mobile 328-742-8268, www.larosadeiventilevanto.com, info@larosadeiventilevanto.com).

Hostel: ¢ Ostello Ospitalia del Mare, a budget gem, is run by the city tourist association. It has 70 basic beds, airy rooms, an elevator, and a terrace in a well-renovated medieval palazzo a few steps from the old town (dorms with private bath and private rooms, includes breakfast, self-service laundry, no curfew, no lockout; office open daily April-Oct 8:00-12:30 & 16:00-19:30, until 23:00 weekend nights; may close Nov-March, Via San Nicolò 1, tel. 0187-802-562, www.ospitaliadelmare.it, info@ospitaliadelmare.it).

Eating in Levanto

$$$ Osteria Tumelin, a local favorite, has a dressy, sophisticated ambience in its elegant dining room, a casual covered terrace out front, and a wide selection of fresh seafood. Reservations are smart on weekends or to dine outside. Check out the aquarium containing giant lobster and moray eels in the first dining room on the right (daily 12:00-14:30 & 19:00-22:30, closed Thu Oct-May, Via D. Grillo 32, across the square from the loggia, tel. 0187-808-379, www.tumelin.it).

$$ Da Rino, a small trattoria on a quiet pedestrian lane, dishes up reasonably priced fresh seafood and homemade Ligurian specialties prepared with care. Consider the grilled *totani* (squid), *pansotti con salsa di noci* (ravioli with walnut sauce), and *trofie al pesto* (local pasta with pesto sauce). Dine indoors or at one of the outdoor tables. On busy nights, they open up a second dining room across the street. Sommelier Anna will help you choose a good wine (Wed-Mon 19:00-22:00, closed Tue, Via Garibaldi 10, tel. 0187-813-475).

$$ Ristorante la Loggia, next to the old loggia, makes fine food, including appealing daily fish specials. Choose between the homey, wood-paneled dining room or the little terrace overlooking the square (daily 12:30-14:00 & 19:00-22:00, closed Nov-Feb, Piazza del Popolo 7, tel. 0187-808-107).

$$$ Ristorante Moresco serves large portions of pasta and seafood at reasonable prices in a vaulted, candlelit room decorated with Moorish-style frescoes. The best value is their €25 four-course tasting menu (drinks extra, 2-person minimum, daily 12:00-14:00 & 19:00-21:00, reservations appreciated, Via Jacopo 24, tel. 0187-807-253, busy Roberto and Francesca).

$$ Taverna Garibaldi, a comfy good-value place on the town's most characteristic street, serves focaccia with various toppings, made-to-order *farinata* (savory chickpea crêpe), salads, and more than 30 types of pizza (Fri-Wed 19:00-22:00, closed Thu, Via Garibaldi 57, tel. 0187-808-098).

$$ La Picea offers prizewinning wood-fired pizzas to go, or you can dine at one of their few small tables (Wed-Sun 19:00-24:00 or until they use up their pizza dough, closed Mon-Tue, just off Piazza Cavour at Via della Concia 18, tel. 0187-802-063).

$$ Pizzeria L'Igea is tucked just inside the Campeggio Acquadolce campground, 50 yards past the hostel. It's a favorite among locals who know you don't have to be a camper to enjoy freshly made, budget-conscious pizza. Their specialty is *gattafin,* deep-fried herb-stuffed ravioli (daily 12:00-14:30 & 18:45-22:30, takeaway available, Via Guido Semenza 5, tel. 0187-807-293).

$ Enoteca La Compera offers a quiet respite on a hidden courtyard across the way from the campground. It's casual and friendly, serving a wide variety of *panini* that you can buy to-go, as well as plenty of wine, including affordable tastings, called *degustazione* (March-Oct daily 10:00-20:00, follow the red-brick road—under the stone arch—to Piazza della Compera 3, mobile 334-712-8517).

Picnics or Bites on the Go: *Focaccerie, rosticcerie,* and delis with takeout pasta abound on Via Dante Alighieri. **$ Focacceria il Falcone** has a great selection of focaccia with different toppings (daily 9:30-22:00, shorter hours off-season, Via Cairoli 19, tel. 0187-807-370). For more picnic options, try the ***mercato*** (mornings except Sun; see "Helpful Hints," page 127). It's fun to grab a crusty loaf of bread, then pair it with a pot of freshly made Genovese pesto and other gifty edibles from **$ Il Laboratorio del Pesto** (daily, Via Dante 14, tel. 0187-807-441).

There are two **Crai supermarkets:** One is just off Piazza Cavour at Via del Municipio 5 (daily 8:00-13:00 & 16:30-20:00); the other is nearby on Piazza Staglieno (similar hours; for a shaded setting, lay out your spread on a bench in the grassy park at this piazza). Another fine picnic spot is Piazza Cristoforo Colombo, located east of the swimming pool, with benches and sea views.

Levanto Connections

From Levanto: To get to the Cinque Terre, you can take the **train** (2-3/hour, 4 minutes to Monterosso). A slower, more scenic option is the **boat,** which stops at every Cinque Terre town—except the hill town of Corniglia—before heading to Porto Venere (April-Sept 2/day at 10:00 and 14:00, price depends on distance—for example, €9 one-way to Vernazza—or get a €32 all-day hop-on, hop-off ticket; only one return boat daily from Porto Venere—departs at about 16:30; get latest boat schedule and price sheet at TI or boat dock or check website, tel. 0187-732-987 or 0187-818-440, www.navigazionegolfodeipoeti.it).

Sestri Levante

This peninsular town is squeezed as skinny as a hot dog between its two beaches. The pedestrian-friendly Corso Colombo, which runs down the middle of the peninsula, is lined with shops that sell takeaway pizza, pastries, and beach paraphernalia.

Hans Christian Andersen enjoyed his visit here in the mid-1800s, writing, "What a fabulous evening I spent in Sestri Levante!" One of the

The Baia del Silenzio beach is ringed by bright, colorful cafés.

bays—Baia delle Favole—is named in his honor (*favole* means "fairy tale"). The small mermaid curled on the edge of the fountain behind the TI is another nod to the beloved Danish storyteller.

Orientation to Sestri Levante

Sestri Levante (pop. 18,000) is dominated by its big, dull modern town in front of the train station. But don't be discouraged—the old town peninsula, a 10-minute walk away, has charm to spare.

Arrival in Sestri Levante: From the train station (no baggage storage), head straight out and across the piazza to go down Via Roma. When you reach the park, turn left and look for the TI in a freestanding kiosk. Nearby, Corso Colombo heads along an enjoyable pedestrian zone to the old town peninsula and beaches.

Tourist Information: It's at Piazza Sant'Antonio 10 (June-Sept daily 10:00-14:00 & 15:00-18:00, shorter hours off-season and closed Mon mornings and all day Sun, tel. 0185-457-011). They can tell you about the local bike-sharing program, and direct you to the trail (south of town) for a 1.5-hour hike (each way) to the scenic Punta Manara promontory.

Market Day: It's on Saturday at Piazza Aldo Moro (8:00-13:00). Also,

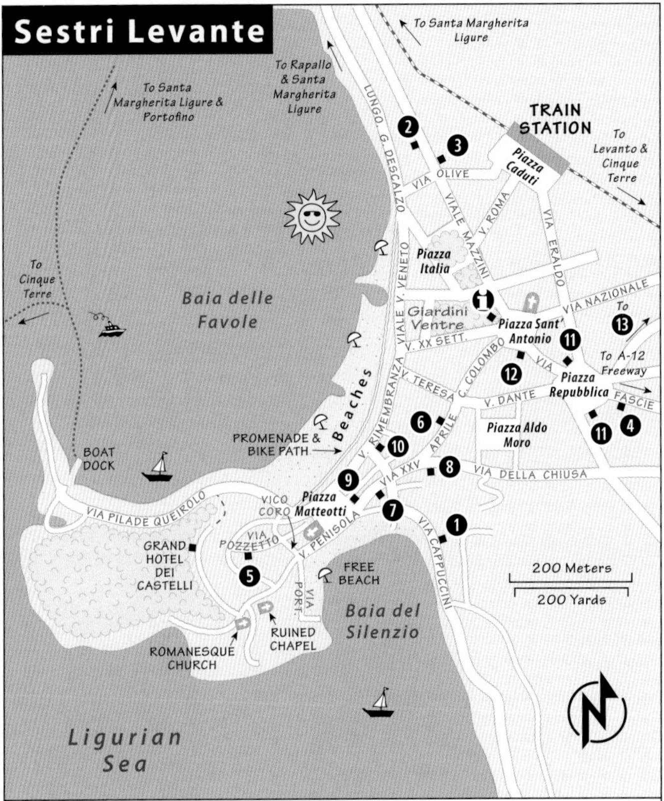

1. Hotel Helvetia
2. Hotel Celeste
3. Hotel Genova
4. Albergo Marina
5. Villa Jolanda
6. L'Osteria Mattana
7. Polpo Mario & Ristorante La Mainolla
8. Ice Cream's Angels
9. Bacciolo Gelato
10. Tama Gelati e Molto di Più
11. Supermarkets (2)
12. Rosticceria Bertolone
13. To Laundrette

local producers of olive oil, cheese, jam, and honey set up on the first and third Saturdays of each month on Via Asilo Maria Teresa (where Via XXV Aprile and Corso Colombo meet).

Laundry: A self-service launderette is in the urban zone southeast of the train station (daily 8:30-20:30, Via Costantino Raffo 8, mobile 389-101-1454).

Sights in Sestri Levante

Stroll the Town

From the TI, take Corso Colombo (to the left of Bermuda Bar, eventually turns into Via XXV Aprile, then Via alla Penisola), which runs up the peninsula. Follow this street—lively with shops, eateries, and delightful pastel facades—for about five minutes. Just before you get to Piazza Matteotti with the large white church at the end, turn off for either beach (free Silenzio beach is on your left). Or continue on the street to the left of the church and head uphill. You'll pass a scenic amphitheater, then the evocative arches of a ruined chapel (bombed during World War II and left as a memorial). A few minutes farther on, past a stony Romanesque church, the road winds to the right to Grand Hotel dei Castelli. The rocky, forested bluff at the end of the town's peninsula is actually the huge private backyard of this fancy hotel.

Beaches

These are named after the bays *(baie)* that they border. The less scenic, bigger beach, **Baia delle Favole,** is divided up much of the year (May-Sept) into sections that you must pay to enter. Fees, up to €30 per day in August, generally include chairs, umbrellas, and fewer crowds. There are several small free sections: at the ends and in the middle (look for *libere* signs, and ask *"Gratis?"* to make sure that it's free). For less expensive sections of beach (where you can rent a chair for about €8-10), ask for *spiaggia libera attrezzata* (spee-AH-jah LEE-behr-ah ah-treh-ZAHT-tah). The usual beach-town activities are clustered along this *baia:* boat rentals, sailing lessons, and bocce courts.

The town's other beach, **Baia del Silenzio,** is picturesque, narrow, virtually all free, and jam-packed, providing a good chance to see Italian families at play. There isn't much more to do here than unroll a beach towel and join in. Because of the bay's small size and the currents, the water gets warmer here than at **Baia delle Favole.** At the far end of Baia del Silenzio (under Hotel Helvetia) is the **$$ Citto Beach bar,** which offers front-row seats with bay views (summer until very late, spring and fall until sunset, sandwiches and salads at lunchtime only, Gilberto).

Sleeping in Sestri Levante

$$$$ Hotel Helvetia, overlooking Baia del Silenzio, feels posh and romantic, with 21 plush rooms, a large sun terrace with a heated, cliff-hanging swimming pool, and a peaceful garden atmosphere. This is a big splurge—with doubles north of €300 in peak season—but it's sure enticing (family rooms, air-con, elevator, shuttle to off-site pay parking, closed Nov-March, Via Cappuccini 43, tel. 0185-41175, www.hotelhelvetia.it, helvetia@hotelhelvetia.it, Alex).

$$$ Hotel Celeste, a dream for beach lovers, rests along the waterfront. Its 41 rooms are modern, crisp, and pricey, but you're paying for the sea breeze (family rooms, air-con, elevator, attached beachside bar/breakfast terrace, Lungomare Descalzo 14, tel. 0185-485-005, www.hotelceleste.com, info@hotelceleste.com, Franco).

$$ Hotel Genova, well-run by the Bertoni family, is a shipshape hotel with 19 shiny-clean, modern, and cheery rooms (three with sea view), a sunny lounge, rooftop sundeck, free loaner bikes, and a good location just two blocks from Baia delle Favole (ask for quieter room in back, family rooms, air-con, elevator, pay parking, Viale Mazzini 126, tel. 0185-41057, www.hotelgenovasestrilevante.com, info@hotelgenovasestrilevante.com, Stefano).

$$ Albergo Marina's friendly Magda and her brother Santo rent 23 peaceful, clean, good-value rooms painted in sea-foam green. Though the hotel is located on a busy boulevard in the more urban part of town, rooms face a quiet back courtyard (family rooms, air-con, elevator, free self-service laundry, pool table, closed Nov-Easter, Via Fasce 100, tel. 0185-41527, www.marinahotel.it, marinahotel@marinahotel.it).

$ Villa Jolanda is a homey, bare-bones *pensione* on the hilly old town streets beyond the pedestrian zone. It has 17 dated rooms (5 with little balconies and territorial views) and a garden courtyard/sun terrace—perfect for families on a budget...and the owner's cats (family rooms, free parking, located near Baia del Silenzio at Via Pozzetto 15, tel. 0185-41354, www.villajolanda.it, info@villajolanda.it, Mario).

Eating in Sestri Levante

Everything listed is on classic Via XXV Aprile, which also abounds with *focaccerie,* takeout pizza by the slice, and little grocery shops. Assemble a picnic or try one of the places below.

At **$$ L'Osteria Mattana,** where everyone shares long tables in two dining rooms (the second one is past the wood oven and brazier), you can mix with locals while enjoying traditional cuisine, listed on chalkboard menus (Mon-Fri 19:30-22:30, Sat-Sun 12:30-14:30 & 19:30-22:30, no dinner served Mon Nov-April, cash only; follow Corso Colombo from TI as it turns into Via XXV Aprile, restaurant on right at #34; tel. 0185-457-633, Marco).

$$$ Polpo Mario is classier, with a fun people-watching location on the main drag (Tue-Sun 12:15-15:00 & 19:00-23:00, closed Mon, Via XXV Aprile 163, tel. 0185-480-203).

$$ Ristorante La Mainolla offers pizzas, big salads, focaccia sandwiches, and reasonably priced pastas near Baia del Silenzio (daily 12:00-16:00 & 19:00-22:00, Via XXV Aprile 187, mobile 338-157-0877, tel. 0185-42792).

Gelato: Tourists flock to **Ice Cream's Angels,** at the intersection of Via XXV Aprile and Via della Chiusa, where Riccardo and Elena artfully load up your cone and top it with a dollop of Nutella chocolate-hazelnut cream (open daily until late in summer). **Bacciolo** enjoys a similar popularity (closed Thu, Via XXV Aprile 51, on the right just before the church). **Tama Gelati e Molto di Più** makes their gelato daily with fresh ingredients (near the beach at Baia delle Favole, Viale Rimembranza 34).

Supermarket: You can stock up on picnic supplies at either **Carrefour Express** branch on Piazza della Repubblica, at #1 (Mon-Sat 8:00-13:00 & 15:30-19:30, closed Sun) or #28 (daily 8:00-24:00).

Deli: For a takeout meal, head to **$ Rosticceria Bertolone** for roasted anything—beef, pork, chicken, or vegetables. Assemble an entire meal from their deli and ask them to heat it for you (Mon-Sat 7:30-13:00 & 16:00-19:30, open Sun mornings in summer but otherwise closed Sun, Via Fascie Vincenzo 12, tel. 0185-487-098).

Sestri Levante Connections

By **train,** Sestri Levante is just 30 minutes from Monterosso (hourly connections with Monterosso; nearly hourly with other Cinque Terre towns, requiring a change in Levanto or Monterosso) and 30 minutes from Santa Margherita Ligure (2/hour).

Boats depart to the Cinque Terre, Porto Venere, Santa Margherita Ligure, Portofino, and San Fruttuoso from the dock *(molo)* on the peninsula (Easter-Oct, tel. 0185-284-670, www.traghettiportofino.it).

Santa Margherita Ligure

If you need the Riviera of movie stars, park your yacht at Portofino. Or you can settle down with more elbow room in nearby and more personable Santa Margherita Ligure (pop. 10,200, one hour by train from the Cinque Terre). While Portofino's velour allure is tarnished by a nonstop traffic jam in peak season, Santa Margherita tumbles easily downhill from its train station. The town has a fun Old World resort character and a breezy harborfront with a beach promenade. With its nice big-city vitality, it feels bustling and lived-in, even off-season.

On a quick day trip to Santa Margherita Ligure from the Cinque Terre or Milan, walk the beach promenade and see the old town center before catching the bus or boat to Portofino to discover what all the fuss is about. With more time, Santa Margherita makes a fine overnight stop or home base for a foray into the Cinque Terre.

Orientation to Santa Margherita Ligure

Arrival by Train: The station is a pleasant, low-stress scene. The bar/café (facing track 1) stores bags (small fee) and sells bus, train, and sightseeing-boat tickets. Enjoy its crazy clocks while you sip an espresso awaiting your train.

To get from the station to the city center, take the stairs marked *Mare* (sea) down to the harbor; or turn right and head more gently down Via Roma, which leads to the town center, TI, start of my town walk, and recommended hotels (about 10 minutes away on foot). Bus #82 to Portofino stops a few steps below the station (2/hour, ticket costs €3 at station bar/café, €5 from driver).

Arrival by Car: Ask your hotelier about parking; some have free spots. Otherwise, try a private lot such as **Autopark,** next to the post office (€15/half-day, €20/24 hours, Via Roma 38, tel. 0185-287-818). An hourly parking lot is by the harbor, in front of the fish market (pay-and-display, €2.50/hour). Parking is generally free where there are white lines; blue lines mean you pay.

Santa Margherita Ligure spills down the hill to its sunny waterfront promenade.

Tourist Information: The TI is as central as can be, at the harborside of the city traffic hub, Piazza Veneto (April-Sept daily 9:30-13:00 & 16:30-19:00, shorter hours off-season, tel. 0185-287-485, www.smlturismo.it). The ATP bus office is next door, and bus #82 to Portofino stops at the curb in front.

Laundry: Close to Piazza Mazzini is **Bolle Blu** (daily 7:00-22:30, Via Roccatagliata 39, mobile 335-642-7203).

Bike Rental and More: GM Rent is at Via XXV Aprile 11 (also rents scooters and Smart Cars, daily 10:00-13:00 & 16:30-20:00, mobile 329-406-6274, www.gmrent.it, Francesco).

Taxi: Taxis wait outside the train station and charge €15 for a ride anywhere in town, €25 to Paraggi beach, and €35 to Portofino (tel. 0185-286-508).

Driver: Helpful taxi driver **Alessandro,** who has five cars and two minivans, offers airport transfers to Genoa, Milan, Florence, and Nice. He is also available for local excursions, including all-day trips to the Cinque Terre (mobile 338-860-2349, www.alessandrotaxi.com, alessandrotaxi@yahoo.it).

Local Guide: Roberta De Beni is good (€100/half-day, €165/day, mobile 349-530-4778, diodebe@inwind.it).

Santa Margherita Ligure Walk

Get your bearings with this little self-guided walk.

▸ *Start at the square facing the exuberant Baroque facade of the Basilica of Santa Margherita.*

Piazza Caprera

Each day this square hosts a few farmers selling their produce. On the corner of Via Cavour, just next to the basilica, visit **Seghezzo,** a recommended, venerable grocer where locals know they'll find whatever they need.

▸ *Now take a side-trip right up the "via principale" (main drag) of the city, Via Palestro/Via Cavour. You'll go two blocks up to Piazza Mazzini and back.*

"Via Principale"

The main "street" here is really two parallel streets divided by very tall, skinny buildings. We'll start by taking Via Cavour (on the left, by Seghezzo grocery) and come back on Via Palestro. As you walk, study the characteristic Art Nouveau house-painting from the turn of the last century. Before

Santa Margherita Ligure

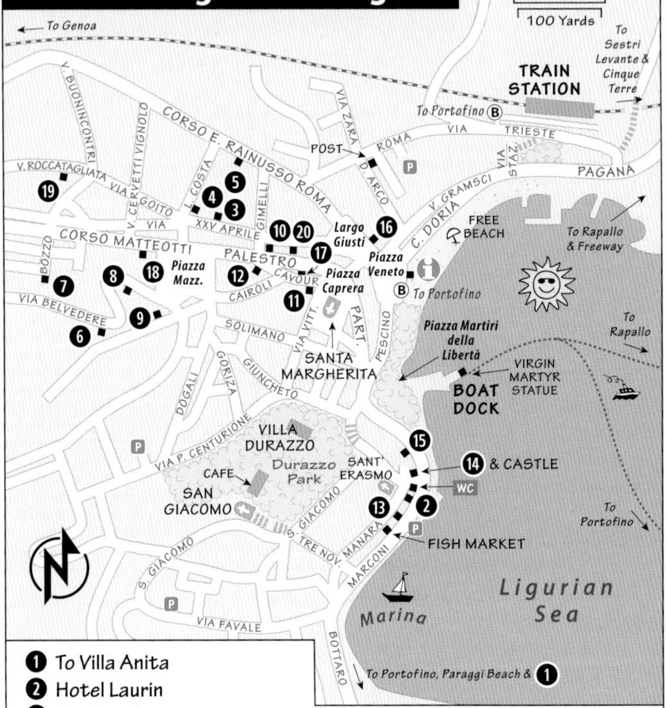

1. To Villa Anita
2. Hotel Laurin
3. Ma Hotel
4. Hotel Jolanda
5. Hotel Tigullio et de Milan
6. Hotel Sant'Andrea
7. Hotel Flory
8. Sabini Rentals
9. Albergo Annabella
10. Angolo 48
11. Vineria Machiavello & Seghezzo Grocery
12. Da Pezzi Ristorante & Pizzeria il Delfino
13. La Cambusa Ristorante
14. Il Vernissage Lounge Bar
15. Simonetti Gelateria
16. Gelateria Centrale
17. Fruttivendolo "Milanese"
18. Co-op Grocery
19. Launderette
20. Bike Rental

1900, people distinguished their buildings with pastel paint and distinctive door and window frames. Then they decided to get fancy and paint entire exteriors with false balconies, weapons, saints, beautiful women, and 3-D Gothic effects.

Strolling up Via Cavour, look through the skinny shops on the right, which also front Via Palestro. Where the two streets merge is the recommended **Angolo 48** restaurant (you might reserve a table for dinner as you pass by).

Continue strolling to the big square, Piazza Mazzini, then do a U-turn to return on Via Palestro toward the big church. At #34 (on the left), you'll pass a traditional ***panificio*** (bakery) where you can say, *"Vorrei un etto di focaccia"* to treat yourself to about a quarter-pound of the region's famed bread (a hearty snack for two). Just beyond, on the right at #13, **Fruttivendolo "Milanese"** sells a staggering variety of tempting produce and glass-jarred delicacies. The sense of family and community all along this stretch is a joy.

▸ *See you back at the church.*

Basilica of Santa Margherita

The town's main church is textbook Italian Baroque (free, daily 7:30-12:00 & 15:00-18:30). Its 18th-century facade hides a 17th-century interior slathered with art and dripping with chandeliers. The altar is typical of 17th-century Ligurian altars—shaped like a boat, with lots of shelf space for candles, flowers, and relics. Its centerpiece is a much venerated statue of Our Lady of the Rose. She's adorned this altar since 1756 and is credited with lots of miracles.

Baroque is theater...and this altar is stagecraft. After the Vatican II decrees of the 1960s, priests began to face their flocks instead of the old altars. For this reason, all over the Catholic world, modern tables serving as post-Vatican II altars stand in front of earlier altars, like the one here, that are no longer the center of attention during Mass.

Wander the church and its chapels, noticing the inlaid-marble floors and sparkling glass chandeliers. As you marvel at the richness, remember that the region's aristocrats amassed wealth from trade from the 11th to the 15th century. When Constantinople fell to the Turks in 1453, free trade in the Mediterranean stopped, and Genovese traders became bankers—making even more money. A popular saying of the day was, "Silver is born in America, lives in Spain, and dies in Genoa." Bankers here served Spain's

The town has pedestrian-friendly squares and an impressive church.

17th-century royalty and aristocracy, and the accrued wealth paid for a Golden Age of art.

▶ *Walk straight in front of the church a block to busy Largo Antonio Giusti. Next to the cinema (across the street), a penguin marks a recommended* gelateria. *Head right to Piazza Veneto, with its busy roundabout and little park on the harbor. In the park facing the roundabout stands the TI, ATP bus office, and a bus #82 stop for Portofino. Use the crosswalks to negotiate the busy intersection and reach the promenade.*

Beachfront Promenade

Stroll to the left along Corso Doria. The sidewalk is wider than the street, an indication that for more than 100 years this has been the place to promenade under century-old pastel facades. You'll pass the grand old **Lido Palace Hotel** with its view balconies overlooking a crowded beach scene.

▶ *Turn around and go back to Piazza Veneto. Continue walking the other direction along the water toward the little castle.*

You'll pass a rack of metal panels limiting political advertising for each party (great idea, wouldn't you say?). Next comes a Christopher Columbus statue. He was born "Cristoforo Colombo" in 1451 in Genoa, near here—although some claim he was Spanish or Portuguese—and first sailed on Genovese boats along this Ligurian coast. Next comes a statue of King Victor Emmanuel II, always ready to brandish his sword and create Italy.

▶ *Before arriving at the castle, head out on the little pier with the white statue facing out to sea.*

View from the Pier

From here, standing with "Santa Margherita Virgin Martyr," you can take in all of Santa Margherita Ligure—from the villas dotting the hills, to the castle built in the 16th century to defend against pirates, to the exclusive hotels. Tourist boats to Portofino, the Cinque Terre, and beyond depart from this pier.

▶ *Continue along the waterfront on Corso Marconi.*

Harbor and Fish Market

Notice the trendy, recommended **Il Vernissage Lounge Bar** with tables up at the base of the castle. Continuing around the corner from the castle (closed to visitors), walk along the harbor. The region's largest fishing fleet—20 boats—ties up here. The fishing industry survives, drag-netting octopus, shrimp, and miscellaneous "blue fish." (Anchovies are no longer fished from here but from nearby Sestri Levante). The **fish market** (Mercato del Pesca, across the street, inside the rust-colored building with arches and columns) wiggles weekdays from about 16:00 until 20:00 or so—depending on who's catching what and when. It's a cool scene as fishermen take bins of freshly caught fish directly to waiting customers.

▶ *Climb the narrow brick stairs just to the right of the fish market to a delightful little square. Find the characteristic, black-and-white pebble mosaic and relax on the benches to enjoy harbor views. Facing the square is the little...*

Oratory of Sant'Erasmo

Named for St. Erasmus, the protector of sailors, this church is actually an "oratory," where a brotherhood of faithful men who did anonymous good deeds congregated and worshipped. While rarely open, do check. The interior is decorated with ships and paintings of storms that local seafarers survived—thanks to St. Erasmus. The huge crosses standing in the nave are carried through town on special religious holidays.

▶ *Your walk is over. For a little extra exercise to see a pleasant park, climb the long stairs from here up to the Church of San Giacomo (with an interior similar to the Basilica of Santa Margherita) and Durazzo Park.*

Sights in Santa Margherita Ligure

Durazzo Park (Parco di Villa Durazzo)

This park is a delight, with a breezy café, a carefully coiffed Italian garden, and an intentionally wild "English garden" below (free, daily 9:00-19:00, until 20:00 July-Aug, closes earlier off-season, WC near café). The Italian garden is famous for its varied collection of palm trees and an extensive collection of camellias. It's OK to feed the large turtles in the central pond (they like bits of fish or meat). The park is dominated by **Villa Durazzo;** it's not worth touring but hosts concerts—mostly in summer.

Beaches

The handiest free beaches are just below the train station toward the boat dock. But the best beaches are on the south side of town, including my favorite, **"Giò e Rino"** (just before Covo di Nord Est)—it's not too expensive, and has a fun, creative management and a youthful crowd. Also nice is the beach on the south side of **Hotel Miramare,** which offers a more relaxing sun-worshipping experience. Both beaches have free entry and rentable chairs and umbrellas. They're a 20-minute walk from downtown, or you can take bus #82 from either the train station or Piazza Veneto (bus tickets-€1.80, €2.80 from driver).

Paraggi, a small ritzy beach halfway to Portofino (and an easy stop on the bus #82 route), is better than any Santa Margherita beach, but it's pricey (as much as €50/day in July and Aug). One Paraggi beach operator,

Enjoying a sunny day on one of Santa Margherita Ligure's beaches.

Bosetti, offers a more reasonable rate (€30/day, includes umbrella, lounge chair, and towel). In high season, the Paraggi beach may be all booked up by big shots from Portofino, which has no beach—only rocks. Off-season, the entire beach is all yours and free of charge. A narrow patch of sand smack-dab in the middle of Paraggi beach is free year-round.

Sleeping in Santa Margherita Ligure

$$$$ Villa Anita is an elegant-yet-homey family hotel run by Daniela and her son, Sandro. They rent 12 tidy rooms—nearly all with terraces and all with high-tech bathrooms—overlooking a peaceful residential neighborhood a five-minute uphill walk from the seaside boulevard. The in-house chef offers a varying menu of Ligurian specialties (dinner extra—not available Mon, family rooms, playground, small gym, small heated pool and sauna, air-con, free parking, closed in winter, Viale Minerva 25, tel. 0185-286-543, www.hotelvillaanita.com, info@hotelvillaanita.com).

$$$$ Hotel Laurin offers slick, modern, air-conditioned, pricey American-style lodgings fixated on harborfront views. All 44 rooms face the sea, most have terraces, and a small pool and gym are on the sundeck. Enrico and staff are helpful (RS%, double-paned windows, elevator, air-con, limited pay parking—request when you reserve, just past the castle, Corso Marconi 3, tel. 0185-289-971, www.laurinhotel.it, info@laurinhotel.it).

$$$ Ma Hotel is a charming, crystal-chandelier-classy boutique hotel with a fresh, modern flair. Although it sits along a busy street, its 11 stylish and spacious rooms are at the back of the building (air-con, patio, free minibar, loaner bikes, Via XXV Aprile 18, tel. 0185-280-224, www.mahotel.it, info@mahotel.it).

$$$ Pastine Hotels: This small chain of well-run hotels combines solid service, sumptuous public spaces, and older rooms. The two main branches are around the corner from each other, an easy walk from the station: **Hotel Jolanda** has lavish public spaces and regal colors, but many of its 50 rooms come with street noise and are getting a bit worn (RS%, air-con, elevator, free use of small weight room, wet and dry saunas, free loaner bikes, Via Luisito Costa 6, tel. 0185-287-512, www.hoteljolanda.it, info@hoteljolanda.it); **Hotel Tigullio et de Milan** is smaller and tidier, with updated rooms (the superior rooms are especially nice and worth a few extra euros) and a rooftop sun terrace with a bar and hot tub in the summer (RS%, air-con, elevator, a few free parking spots, free loaner bikes, Via Rainusso 3, tel. 0185-287-455, www.hoteltigullio.eu, info@hoteltigullio.eu). The newest branch, the boutique-y **Hotel Sant'Andrea,** has 12 rooms near Piazza Mazzini (RS%, air-con, elevator, free parking, Via Belvedere 10, mobile 366-661-8616, www.hotelsantandrea.net, info@hotelsantandrea.net).

$$ Hotel Flory, spanning two buildings surrounded by flowers and greenery, is an old-school hotel with 16 dated rooms and thin walls. It's run enthusiastically by Florinda (who wants to practice her English with you) and Enrico, whose three kids make this a family-friendly place (family rooms, some rooms have balconies, cheaper rooms with private bath down the hall, small public patio, fans, no elevator, rooftop terrace, free loaner bikes, laundry service, pay parking, Via Bozzo 3, tel. 0185-286-435, www.hotelflory.it, hotelflory@hotelflory.it).

$$ Sabini Rentals, in a dull residential zone, offers three straightforward rooms and one apartment with a tiny corner kitchen (RS%, family rooms, 2-night minimum, cash only, Via Belvedere 31, mobile 338-902-7582, www.sabinirentals.com, info@sabinirentals.com, Cristina and Giancarlo).

$ Albergo Annabella is an old-style budget throwback, with nine basic rooms. The **$$** rooms with bathrooms and air-conditioning are overpriced, but the **$** rooms with shared bath and fans are a solid budget option (family rooms, no breakfast, Via Costasecca 10, mobile 380-328-0542, tesibruno@gmail.com, Annabella speaks limited English).

Eating in Santa Margherita Ligure

In the City Center

$$$ Angolo 48, run by savvy Elisa and Valentina, serves beautifully presented and reasonably priced Genovese and Ligurian dishes. At this cool-without-the-pretense locale, reservations are important; there's great seating both on the square and inside. Try their handmade *pansotti* in walnut sauce (lunch served Wed and Sat-Sun 12:00-13:45, dinner nightly 18:30-22:00, Via Palestro 48, tel. 0185-286-650).

$$ Vineria Machiavello feels more urban Tuscan than seaside Ligurian. This well-stocked *enoteca* (wine shop) offers tastings and full bottles, but also serves a short, enticing menu of well-priced dishes at a few humble tables tucked between the wine racks. The menu, which goes beyond seafood and pesto, is a nice break from the Riviera rut (Wed-Mon

10:00-14:00 & 17:30-24:00, closed Tue, in the heart of the pedestrian zone at Via Cavour 17, tel. 0185-286-122).

$$ Da Pezzi, with a cheap cafeteria-style atmosphere, is packed with locals at midday and at night. They're munching *farinata* (crêpes made from chickpeas, available Oct-May 18:00-20:00) standing at the bar, or enjoying pesto and fresh fish in the dining room. Consider the deli counter with its Genovese picnic ingredients (Sun-Fri 10:00-14:00 & 17:00-21:00, table service after 12:00 and 18:00, closed Sat, Via Cavour 21, tel. 0185-285-303, Giancarlo and Giobatta).

On the Waterfront

All along the harbor side of Via Tommaso Bottaro, south of the marina, you'll find restaurants, pizzerias, and bars serving food with a nautical view. These places are a notch above.

$$$ La Cambusa, perched above the fish market, is popular for its seafood. While the food is forgettable, the view from its harborside terrace is not. In cooler weather, the terrace is covered and heated. Diners receive a free glass of *sciacchetrà* (dessert wine) and biscotti with this book (daily 12:00-15:00 & 19:00-24:00 except closed Thu Oct-June, Via Tommaso Bottaro 1, tel. 0185-287-410, www.ristorantelacambusa.net).

At **$$ Il Vernissage Lounge Bar,** you can nurse your €8 drink with a million-dollar view. There are 20 wines by the glass, plus cocktails and spritzes, which always come with a nice plate of finger food (March-Oct daily 18:00-late, Sun from 11:00, Salita al Castello 8, mobile 349-220-5846, Sandro).

Budget Options

$$ Pizzeria il Delfino, which serves thin, big, wood-fired pizzas, offers a rustic, fun local scene, with a few quiet tables outside and tight inside seating under nautical bric-a-brac (daily 12:00-15:00 & 18:00-23:00 except closed Tue dinner, Via Cavour 29, tel. 0185-286-488).

Gelato: The best *gelateria* I found in town—with chocolate-truffle *tartufato*—is **Simonetti** (under the castle at Piazza Martiri della Libertà 48). **Gelateria Centrale,** just off Piazza Veneto near the cinema, serves up their specialty—*pinguino* (penguin), a cone with your choice of gelato dipped in chocolate (Largo Antonio Giusti 14).

Groceries: Classy **Seghezzo** is great for a meal to go—ask them to *riscaldare* (heat up) their white *lasagne al pesto* or dish up their special *carpaccio di polpo*—thinly sliced octopus (daily June-Aug 7:30-13:00 & 15:30-20:00, closed Wed Sept-May, right of the church on Via Cavour, tel. 0185-287-172). The **Co-op** grocery, off Piazza Mazzini, is cheaper and less romantic (daily 8:15-13:00 & 15:30-19:30 except closed Sun afternoon, Corso Giacomo Matteotti 9). Either is a good place to stock up on well-priced Ligurian olive oil, pasta, and pesto.

Santa Margherita Ligure Connections

To reach the **Cinque Terre** towns (beyond Monterosso), you'll usually have to change in Sestri Levante, Levanto, or Monterosso.

From Santa Margherita Ligure by Train to: Sestri Levante (2/hour, 30 minutes), **Monterosso** (hourly, 45 minutes), **La Spezia** (hourly, 1-1.5 hours), **Pisa** (1-2/hour, 2 hours, most with transfer, less frequent InterCity/IC goes direct), **Florence** (8/day, 4 hours, transfer in Pisa), **Milan** (about hourly, 2.5 hours, more with transfer in Genoa), **Ventimiglia**/French border (4/day, 4 hours; or hourly with change in Genoa), **Venice** (at least hourly, 6 hours with changes).

By Boat to the Cinque Terre: Tour boats make various trips to Vernazza, Porto Venere, and other ports nearly every day. Pick up a schedule of departures and excursion options from the TI, visit the ticket shack on the dock, call 0185-284-670, or check www.traghettiportofino.it.

Portofino

Santa Margherita Ligure, with its aristocratic architecture, hints at old money. But nearby Portofino (pop. 500)—with its sleek jewelry shops, art galleries, and haute couture boutiques filling a humble village shell—has the sheen of new money. It's the kind of place where the sailing masts are taller than the houses and church steeples. But the *piccolo* harbor, classic Italian architecture, and wooded peninsula turn glitzy Portofino into an appealing destination, rated ▲▲. Just a couple of miles down the coast, it's a fun, easy day trip from Santa Margherita Ligure.

Planning Your Time: My favorite Portofino plan is to visit in the late afternoon. Leave Santa Margherita by bus at about 16:30, get off at Paraggi beach, and hike 30 minutes over the bluff into Portofino. Explore the town, splurge for a drink on the harborfront, or get a takeout fruity sundae (*paciugo;* pah-CHOO-goh) and sit by the water. Then return by bus

Popular with celebrities, Portofino is a classic Riviera beach town: pricey and pretty.

to Santa Margherita for dinner (confirm late departures). If you plan to do some hiking around Portofino, come earlier in the day.

Getting to Portofino

You can reach Portofino from Santa Margherita by bus or boat, or on foot. For a fun combination, you could go one way by boat, and the other via bus and on foot from Paraggi. (I wouldn't bike it, due to the blind corners.)

By Bus: Catch bus #82 from Santa Margherita's train station or at bus stops along the harbor (main stop in front of TI, €3 one-way or €4 from driver, €5 round-trip, 2/hour—hourly on Sun, 15 minutes, goes to Paraggi beach and then to Portofino). Buy tickets at the train station bar; at Piazza Veneto's green bus kiosk or the nearby green ticket machine (next to the TI); or at any newsstand, tobacco shop, or shop that displays a *Biglietti Bus* sign. If you're at the Piazza Veneto kiosk, grab a bus schedule to plan your return (last bus around 23:00, earlier on Sun).

By Boat and Bus: If you're arriving in Portofino by boat, but will be busing back, follow the narrow lanes up from the harbor to find Piazza della Libertà and the bus stop (ticket machine on right; tobacco store on left also sells tickets).

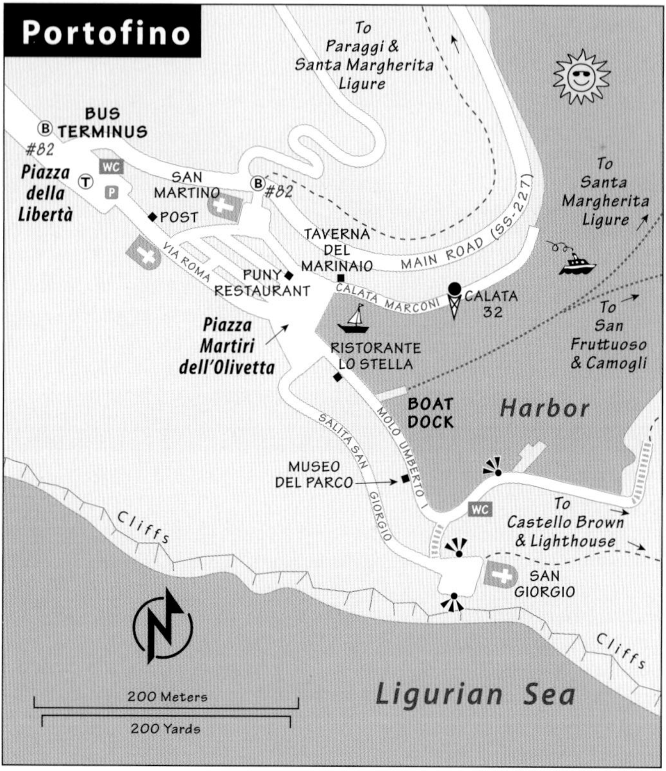

By Taxi: A taxi from Santa Margherita will cost around €35 to Portofino or €25 to Paraggi beach. (Taxi stands in Santa Margherita are at the train station and down by the water on Via Pescino, not far from the TI.)

By Boat: The boat makes the 15-minute trip with more class and scenery, and without the traffic jams. The dock in Santa Margherita is off Piazza Martiri della Libertà, a two-minute walk from Piazza Veneto (€6.50 one-way, €9.50 round-trip; hourly departures April-Oct daily 10:15-16:15, fewer off-season; tel. 0185-284-670, www.traghettiportofino.it).

On Foot: To hike from Santa Margherita Ligure to Portofino, you have two options: You can follow the sidewalk along (and sometimes hanging over) the sea (1 hour, 2.5 miles)—although traffic can be noisy, and in places, the footpath disappears. Or, if you're hardy and ambitious, you can take a quieter two-hour hike by leaving Santa Margherita at Via Maragliano, then follow the Ligurian-symbol trail markers (keep a close eye out for red-and-white stripes). This hike takes you high into the hills. Keep left after Cappelletta delle Gave. Several blocks past a castle, you'll drop down into the Paraggi beach, where you'll take the Portofino trail the rest of the way.

Bus-and-Hike Option: For a shorter—but rewarding—30-minute hike into Portofino, ride bus #82 from Santa Margherita only as far as Paraggi beach. (Ask on board where to get off—watch for an inland bay with green water and a sandy beach.) At the far end of the beach, cross the street, climb the steps, and follow the hilly, paved trail marked *Pedonale per Portofino* high above the road. There's a fair amount of up and down, but it's all well-paved and scenic. After Paraggi, you'll curl around another bay—with the famously top-end Hotel Splendido hovering on the hill above—before snaking your way to Portofino.

Sights in Portofino

▲▲Self-Guided Visual Tour from the Harbor

Stand or sit on the angled boat launch where Piazza Martiri dell'Olivetta meets the harbor (or nurse an overpriced cocktail at the nearby café tables), and get oriented to Portofino. It's one of the Mediterranean's most beautiful and famous little resorts.

Scanning the humble houses around the harbor, notice the painted-on details—as in Santa Margherita Ligure. You may also see laundry hanging out to dry—a jarring reminder that, while Ferragamo and Prada may reside on street level, actual villagers still live upstairs.

Now look out to the well-protected natural harbor—which has held substantial strategic value ever since the Romans first founded a town here. Since then, it has been appreciated by everyone from Napoleon to the Nazis.

A new flock of fans arrived in the 1950s, when *National Geographic* ran a beautiful article on the idyllic port. Locals claim that's when the Hollywood elite took note. Liz Taylor and Richard Burton came here annually (as did Liz Taylor and Eddie Fisher). During one famous party, Rex Harrison dropped his Oscar into the bay (it was recovered). Ava Gardner came down from her villa each evening for a drink—sporting her famous fur coat. Greta Garbo loved to swim naked in the harbor, not knowing (or caring) that half the town was watching. Truman Capote also called Portofino home. But VIPs were also here a century earlier. Friedrich Nietzsche famously wrote about philosophizing with the mythical prophet Zarathustra on the path between Portofino and Santa Margherita.

Today, the celebrity cachet lives on. When you tell locals you're going to Portofino, they say, "Maybe you'll see George Clooney!" Count the yachts and the tall-masted sailboats, and imagine who might be on them.

Now scan the panorama on the hillside in front of you. On the left is **Castello Brown,** an actual medieval castle built by the Genovese in the 16th century to protect this strategic harbor. It later became a private mansion, and today is a museum featuring lush gardens, sweeping viewpoints, and exhibits about Portofino and its history (€5, daily June-Aug 10:00-19:00, April-May and Sept-Oct until 18:00, shorter hours off-season, tel. 0185-267-101, www.castellobrown.com).

Panning right, you'll see the **Church of San Giorgio,** with its popular viewpoint terrace looking down over the port and out over the ocean. This is an easy option for a hike with grand views. Boats back to Portofino depart from the harborfront below this church. The Museo del Parco (described next) is also along this embankment.

Now look back toward town. A tidy grid of narrow cobbled streets angles gently uphill to the modern part of town, around Piazza Martiri della Libertà (where you'll find the bus stop back to Santa Margherita Ligure). These streets—where budget takeaway eateries and grocery stores are mixed in with swanky shops—are a good place to hunt for picnic fare. Up on the right is the striped church of San Martino, marking the well-manicured, enjoyable 30-minute trail to Paraggi beach.

Museo del Parco

For an artsy break, walk around the harbor to the right, where you can stroll around a park littered with 148 contemporary sculptures by mostly Italian artists, including a few top names (€5, June-Sept Wed-Mon 10:00-13:30 & 15:00-20:00; closed Tue, off-season, and in bad weather; mobile 337-333-737).

Hikes

The **Parco di Portofino** can provide detailed information on the many hiking trails that crisscross Portofino's regional parklands (tel. 0185 289-479,

On the way to or from Portofino, stop for a dip at Paraggi beach.

www.parcoportofino.it). Here are two options easily accessible from Portofino itself.

Lighthouse Hike: A paved stone path winds up and down to the lighthouse *(faro)* at the scenic point beyond the Church of San Giorgio. Take the stairs on the right just after Museo del Parco, and keep going past the church. Hedges block views until the end, when you'll be rewarded with the open sea—and a lounge/bar (open May-Sept, 25-minute walk). Consider popping into the medieval Castello Brown on the way up or down.

Paraggi Beach Hike: You can stroll the hilly pedestrian promenade through the trees from Portofino to Paraggi beach, and, if you're lucky, see a wild boar en route (30 minutes, path starts to the right of striped Divo Martino church just above the harborfront piazza, and ends at ritzy Paraggi beach, where bus #82 stops on its way back to Santa Margherita Ligure—though in peak season, the bus can get filled up in Portofino).

Eating in Portofino

Portofino offers all kinds of harborside dining, but the quality often doesn't match the high prices. I'd rather dine in Santa Margherita Ligure. But if you do eat in Portofino, **$$$ Ristorante lo Stella,** just a few steps from the boat dock, has well-prepared dishes, friendly servers, and portholes in the bathrooms. **$$$ Taverna del Marinaio,** across the harbor, has a prime location (soaking up the last of the day's sun), tables under arcades, and a small, cozy, classy interior. And **$$$$ Puny,** at the top of the harborfront square, is a famous splurge (reserve ahead, 0185-269-037).

For budget options, you'll find a variety of *foccacerie,* pizzerias, and grocery stores hiding out in the tiny grid of streets just up from the water. For dessert, opposite the boat dock, little **Calata 32** is well-regarded for its gelato.

South of the Cinque Terre

South of the Cinque Terre is the nothing-special town of La Spezia, a handy transit hub with excellent train connections. But nearby is a gem—the resort town of Porto Venere, worthy of a day trip by boat from the Cinque Terre or by bus from La Spezia.

Porto Venere

The perfect antidote to gritty La Spezia hides just around the bay: the enchanting resort of Porto Venere (POR-toh VEH-neh-reh). Comparably scenic to the Cinque Terre towns—but with a bit of glitz—this village clings to a rocky, fortress-crowned promontory. A rainbow of tall, skinny pastel facades rises up from an inviting harborfront promenade.

Porto Venere is light on sights, but it's a breeze to reach by boat from the Cinque Terre, and fun to explore: The higher you go, the better the views. Rather than the open sea, Porto Venere faces the beautiful Gulf of La Spezia—more romantically known as the Gulf of Poets—where Lord Byron was said to have gone for a hardy swim despite rough seas and local warnings to the contrary. (He survived...at least, for a little while longer.) Scanning the bay, you'll see the outskirts of muscular La Spezia, the often-snow-covered peaks of the Apuan Alps, the resort town of Lerici, and—across a narrow strait—the rugged island of Palmaria.

Orientation to Porto Venere

Getting There: Porto Venere is an easy day trip from the Cinque Terre towns by **boat** (mid-June-Oct, 4/day, 1 hour from Monterosso, €16 one-way, €30 day pass includes hopping on and off, www.navigazionegolfodeipoeti.it). You can also cruise between Porto Venere and Santa Margherita Ligure, with stops in Vernazza and Sestri Levante, using another boat line (www.traghettiportofino.it)—see page 152. The scenic **bus** ride between La Spezia and Porto Venere curls around the Gulf of Poets (see page 164).

For **drivers,** parking is challenging. In peak season, shuttle buses connect the parking lot just outside Porto Venere to the harborside square. Otherwise, test your luck with the pay spots on the seaside.

Lovely Porto Venere offers grand views to hikers and a harborfront promenade.

Tourist Information: The TI fills an old guard tower at the top of the main square (Piazza Bastreri 7, tel. 0187-790-691, www.prolocoportovenere.it).

Visiting Porto Venere

The town is essentially two streets deep: the harborfront promenade and, a block uphill, the main street (Via Capellini). A complete loop around Porto Venere includes both of these streets and a moderately steep hike up to the town's two main churches and fortress for the views. You can see everything in just a few hours; add more time for lunch or lingering.

Along the **harborfront,** seafood restaurants enjoy a Technicolor backdrop, and boat captains try to talk you into a 40-minute excursion around the bay. But the real town lives on **Via Capellini** (just through the big arch from the TI—or hike up any of the narrow stepped lanes from the harbor). Skinny and shaded, Via Capellini has a mix of restaurants, focaccia-and-pizza takeaway stands, several local shops, and boutiques selling gourmet gifty edibles and gaudy beachwear.

At the west end of the promenade and Via Capellini, the town comes

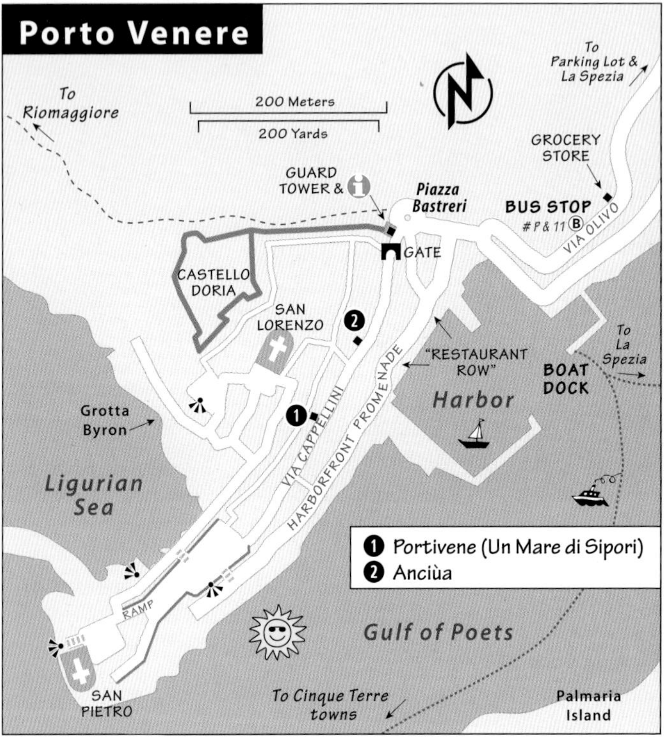

to a point at the late 13th-century **Church of San Pietro,** with Gothic features and a black-and-white-striped interior typical of this region. Climb the stairs to the roof terrace for fine views in both directions (including the "Grotta Byron" sea cave).

More viewpoints line the walk from here up the stairs to the town's other big church, **San Lorenzo.** With a dark and brooding Romanesque interior, this church—like much of Porto Venere—was built by the Genovese to establish a strategic foothold at the entrance to the bay in the 12th century.

From in front of the church, more steps lead up to the town's fortress,

Porto Venere's narrow lanes offer a mix of shops and restaurants.

Castello Doria. A hulking shell, it's not worth the money to go inside, but a hike up to the terrace out front is rewarded with striking panoramas.

From the castle, head back into town; to make this walk a loop, bear left to follow the very steeply stepped lane that runs just inside the crenellated wall back down to the TI.

Hardy **hikers** enjoy the five-hour (or more) hike to Riomaggiore, the nearest Cinque Terre town. Get details on this and other hikes at the TI; for more on hiking the Cinque Terre, see page 23.

Eating in Porto Venere

On the harbor, next to colorful bobbing boats, take your pick of views and menus (seafood/pizza) for a meal in a memorable setting.

For better values and more variety, stroll one block inland to Via Capellini. For a sit-down meal along here, try **$$ Portivene (Un Mare di Sipori),** serving local dishes with modern flair at reasonable prices (reservations smart, closed Mon, at #94, tel. 0187-792-722). Better yet, browse the fun selection of takeaway shops (selling pizza slices, bruschetta, focaccia, and top-notch deli items) to put together a picnic to enjoy by the port. **$ Anciùa** (at #40) assembles *panini* to order with interesting ingredients; they also have fresh fried anchovies and other Ligurian street food.

La Spezia

While just a quick train ride south of the fanciful Cinque Terre (20-30 minutes), the working city of La Spezia (pop. 94,000) feels like "reality Italy." Primarily a transit point connecting to the Cinque Terre, lovely Porto Venere, or to Pisa, Lucca, and other Tuscan towns, La Spezia is slim on sights and has no beaches. In recent years, La Spezia has become the entry point for big cruise ships that funnel groups into the Cinque Terre.

Orientation to La Spezia

Arrival in La Spezia: The La Spezia Centrale train station has various services lined up along track 1; at the Cinque Terre end are pay WCs and luggage storage (€3/day, 8:00-22:00—if nobody's there ring the bell). In the middle of the platform is a Cinque Terre National Park information point, where you can buy park tickets—including the Cinque Terre Treno Multi-Service Card that includes both trains and trails (daily 7:30-19:30, off-season 9:00-17:30, tel. 0187-743-500, www.parconazionale5terre.it). Don't use the La Spezia Migliarina station, where some trains terminate, which is more remote.

For **drivers,** the easiest parking is under the train station, at the slick and modern Park Centro Stazione (enter from Via Fiume, €18/day, www.mobpark.eu/it/). Free parking is at Piazza d'Armi, a 20-minute walk or short bus ride from the station (entrance at Via XV Giugno 1918).

Visiting La Spezia

If you find yourself with extra time here, and would like a meal, a museum stop, or a stroll, here's how to accomplish all three: Exit the station, turn left, and walk a long downhill block (on Via Paleocapa Pietro) to the roundabout at Piazza Saint Bon, which marks the start of a pleasant pedestrian zone—with several eateries—on **Via Fiume** (which turns into **Via del Prione).** Continuing on this street to the harborfront gardens makes a nice stroll (it's one mile from station to harbor). Along the way,

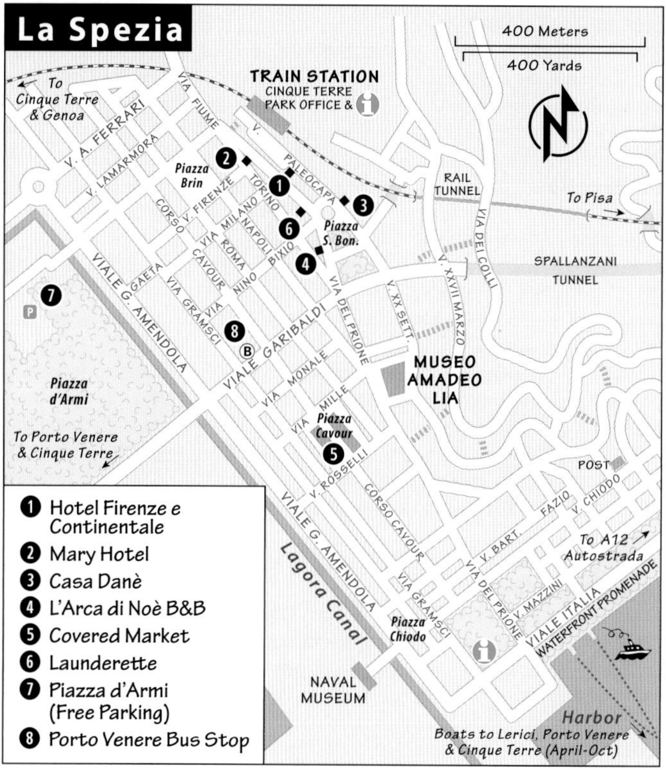

you'll pass the nearly deserted **Museo Amedeo Lia,** which displays Italian paintings from the 13th to 18th century, including minor works by Venetian masters Titian, Tintoretto, and Canaletto (tel. 0187-731-100, http://museolia.spezianet.it).

Without a doubt, the most appealing sight is outside of La Spezia: **Porto Venere,** a gorgeous Cinque Terre-esque town overlooking a beautiful bay, is just a 30-minute bus ride away (see "La Spezia Connections" next page).

Sleeping in La Spezia

Stay in the Cinque Terre if you can, but if you're in a bind, these accommodations are within a 10-minute walk of the station: **$$$$ Hotel Firenze e Continentale** is your grand, Old World splurge (68 rooms, RS%, air-con, elevator, pay parking garage, Via Paleocapa 7, tel. 0187-713-200 or 0187-713-210, www.hotelfirenzecontinentale.it, info@hotelfirenzecontinentale.it). **$$ Mary Hotel,** directly across from the train station, has 48 basic, old-school rooms (air-con, elevator, Via Fiume 177, tel. 0187-743-254, www.hotelmary.it, info@hotelmary.it, friendly Luca).

For *affittacamere* rooms for rent, consider the stylish **$ Casa Danè** (10 chic rooms with comfy linens and orange trees outside the door, plus 20 more rooms inside the station building itself, some rooms overlook the tracks but the windows are good, family rooms, air-con, Via Paleocapa 4, mobile 347-351-3239, www.casadane.it, reception@casadane.it, Paolo), or the homey **$ L'Arca di Noè B&B** (three bright, artsy, affordable rooms—two with bathroom inside the room, the other with private bath down the hall; air-con, communal kitchen, Via Fiume 39, mobile 320-485-2434, montialessandra@email.it, Alessandra).

A handy self-service **launderette** is just below the train station (daily 8:30-20:30, Via Fiume 95).

La Spezia Connections

Trains leave about twice hourly for the **Cinque Terre towns** (direction: Levanto). A few express trains (headed to Genoa or Milano) stop only at Monterosso. Other connections include **Pisa** (about hourly, 1 hour), **Florence** (5/day direct, 2.5 hours, otherwise nearly hourly with change in Pisa), **Rome** (8/day direct, more with transfers in Pisa, 3-4.5 hours), **Milan** (about hourly, 3 hours direct or with change in Genoa), **Venice** (about hourly, 5-6 hours, 1-3 changes).

It's also possible to go by **boat** to the Cinque Terre, Porto Venere, and outer islands from the La Spezia dock (www.navigazionegolfodeipoeti.it).

City **buses to Porto Venere** generally depart from Viale Garibaldi; the bus stop is about a 10-minute walk from the train station (see map on page 163 for location; bus #P, 2/hour, 30 minutes, €2.50 each way; bus #11 also makes the trip, but only mid-June-mid-Sept and sporadically off-season; buy tickets at TI, tobacco shops, or newsstands).

Practicalities

Time your trip to avoid crowds, or explore towns early or late in the day.

PLANNING

Spring through fall is peak season in the Cinque Terre, with the best weather and the most crowds. Book rooms ahead, especially during the peak of the peak times: holidays (including Easter and Italian Liberation Day on April 25), May, June, all summer weekends, and September.

In spring, the Cinque Terre can feel packed with day-tripping Italian families and school groups. July and August are hotter and generally a bit less crowded. The winter is dead—most hotels and some restaurants close from January to March.

Make sure your passport is up to date (to renew, see www.travel.state.gov). Call your debit- and credit-card companies about your plans. Consider buying travel insurance. If you're traveling beyond the Cinque Terre, research rail passes, train reservations, and car rentals. For information on all of these topics and much more, including updates to this book, see www.ricksteves.com.

MONEY

Italy uses the euro currency: 1 euro (€) = about $1.10. To convert prices in euros to dollars, add about 10 percent: €20 = about $22, €50 = about $55. (Check www.oanda.com for the latest exchange rates.)

Withdraw money from a cash machine (called a *bancomat* in Italy) using a debit card, just like at home.

Visa and MasterCard are commonly used throughout Europe. Before departing, call your bank or credit-card company: Ask about international

Useful Websites and Contacts

Tourist Information: For all of Italy, see www.italia.it. For the Cinque Terre: www.cinqueterre.it; for the Cinque Terre National Park: www.parconazionale5terre.it.
Passports and Red Tape: www.travel.state.gov
Cheap Flights: www.kayak.com (for international flights), www.skyscanner.com (for flights within Europe)
Airplane Carry-on Restrictions: www.tsa.gov
European Train Schedules: www.bahn.com
General Travel Tips: www.ricksteves.com

Contacts in Italy

Police, Fire, and Ambulance (Europe-wide): Tel. 112
Italian State Police: Tel. 113
Ambulance: Tel. 118
Road Service: Tel. 116
US Embassy in Rome: 24-hour emergency line—tel. 06-46741, nonemergency—tel. 06-4674-2420 (by app't only, Via Vittorio Veneto 121, http://italy.usembassy.gov)
US Consulates in Milan—tel. 02-290-351 (Via Principe Amedeo 2/10, http://milan.usconsulate.gov); **in Florence**—tel. 055-266-951 (Lungarno Vespucci 38, http://florence.usconsulate.gov)
Canadian Embassy in Rome: Tel. 06-854-442-911 (Via Zara 30, www.italy.gc.ca)
Canadian Consulate in Milan: Tel. 02-626-94238 (Piazza Cavour 3, www.italy.gc.ca)

transaction fees, and alert them that you'll be making withdrawals in Europe. Many travelers bring a second debit/credit card as a backup. Cash is always good to have on hand, so try to withdraw large amounts of euros (€250-300) from the ATM.

While American credit cards are accepted almost everywhere in Europe, even newer chip-style cards may not work in some automated payment machines (e.g., ticket kiosks). Be prepared to pay with cash, find

Theft and Emergencies

Theft Alert: Any commotion in a crowd can be a smokescreen for pickpockets, and distracted tourists make easy targets. Wear a money belt (tucked under your beltline) to hide your valuables—passport, credit cards, crucial documents, and large amounts of cash.

If you lose your credit or debit card, report the loss immediately. Call these 24-hour US numbers collect: Visa (tel. 303/967-1096), MasterCard (tel. 636/722-7111), and American Express (tel. 336/393-1111). In Italy, to make a collect call to the US, dial 800-172-444.

To replace a passport, contact an embassy or consulate (for contact info, see page 167). File a police report without delay; it's required to submit an insurance claim for lost or stolen rail passes or travel gear, and can help with replacing your passport or credit and debit cards. For more info, see www.ricksteves.com/help.

Medical Emergencies: Dial 112 for English-speaking police/medical emergencies, or 118 for an ambulance. If you get a minor ailment, do as the Italians do and go to a pharmacy, where qualified technicians routinely diagnose and prescribe. Or ask at your hotel for help—they'll know the nearest medical and emergency services.

a nearby cashier, or try entering your credit card's PIN (though you'll need to get the PIN from your bank before your trip).

Tipping

Tipping in Europe isn't as automatic and generous as it is in the US. To tip a taxi driver, round up to the nearest euro (for a €5.50 fare, give €6), or up to 10 percent for longer rides. You don't have to tip at restaurants because service is often included, but if you tip for good service, add a euro or two per person at your table; for more, see page 173.

Shopping, VAT Refunds, and Customs

The Cinque Terre has limited options for shoppers, such as tacky (if fun) beach trinkets and T-shirts. Some of the towns have higher-quality art boutiques. But in general, the Cinque Terre's best souvenirs are edible: a jar of pesto; dried *trofie* pasta to go with it; olive oil; the sweet *sciacchetrà* dessert wine; and lemon-flavored or -scented goods (since Liguria is one of just two places in Italy with serious lemon production).

Getting a VAT Refund: If you spend more than €155 on goods at a single store, you may be eligible to get a refund of the 22 percent Value-Added Tax (VAT). Have the store fill out the paperwork; you'll need to show them your passport. At the airport, get your papers stamped by customs *before* going through security, then process your refund through a service such as Global Blue or Premier Tax Free (for details, see www.ricksteves.com/vat).

Customs for American Shoppers: You're allowed to take home $800 worth of items and one liter of alcohol per person duty-free. You can take home many processed and packaged foods (e.g., vacuum-packed cheeses, chocolate) but no fresh produce or meats. Any liquid-containing foods must be packed (carefully) in checked luggage. To check customs rules and duty rates, visit help.cbp.gov.

HELPFUL HINTS

Hurdling the Language Barrier: Most people in the tourist industry—and nearly all young people—speak some English. Still, learn the pleasantries such as *buon giorno* (good day), *per favore* (please), *grazie* (thank you), *mi scusi* (pardon me), and *arrivederci* (goodbye). For more phrases, see page 179.

Time Zones: Italy is generally six/nine hours ahead of the East/West coasts of the US. For a time converter, try www.timeanddate.com/worldclock.

Business Hours: Small-town Italy often observes the siesta plan (stores open Mon-Sat 9:00-13:00 & 15:30-19:30), though in tourist areas, larger shops may be open through lunch and also on Sunday.

Watt's Up? Europe's electrical system is 220 volts, instead of North America's 110 volts. You'll need an adapter plug with two round prongs, sold inexpensively at travel stores in the US. Most newer electronics (such as mobile devices, laptops, hair dryers, and battery chargers) convert automatically, so you won't need a separate converter.

Numbers and Stumblers: What Americans call the second floor of a building is the first floor in Europe. Europeans write dates as day/month/year (Christmas is 25/12). Commas are decimal points and vice versa—a dollar and a half is 1,50, and there are 5.280 feet in a mile.

Italy uses the metric system: A kilogram is 2.2 pounds; 100 grams (*un etto,* a common unit of sale at markets) is about a quarter-pound. A liter is about a quart, and a kilometer is six-tenths of a mile (50 km = 30 miles).

Temperature is measured in Celsius (0°C = 32°F). To roughly convert Celsius to Fahrenheit, double the number and add 30. 28°C = 82°F. For health, 37°C is just right. At a launderette, 30°C is cold, 40°C is warm (default setting), and 60°C is hot. When using air-conditioning, 21°C is a comfortable setting.

SLEEPING

I've rated my recommended accommodations with a price code to help you find a place that meets your budget (see page 8).

On the Cinque Terre

Vernazza, the spindly and salty essence of the Cinque Terre, is my top choice for a home base. And its new summer opera series has beefed up its nightlife. But if you think too many people have my book, you'll get fewer crowds and better value for your money in other towns.

Monterosso is a good choice for sun-worshipping beach lovers, those who prefer the ease of a real hotel, and a younger crowd interested in nightlife.

Manarola, charming and not overrun, draws serious hikers and sophisticated Europeans. The town has a good range of professional-feeling small accommodations, but fewer dining or evening options.

Events in the Cinque Terre

Book your room ahead if your visit coincides with a popular event. For festival info and to confirm dates, check CinqueTerre.it and Turismoin-Liguria.it (food festivals in particular are subject to change). Many sights and banks close down on national holidays.

Easter Sunday and Monday	**Popular time to visit the Cinque Terre** (book ahead)
April 25	**Italian Liberation Day** (avoid this day, as locals literally shut down the trails)
May 1	**Labor Day** (Cinque Terre gets packed with day-trippers)
Mid-May (third Sat)	**Monterosso: Lemon Festival**
Mid-June (third Sat)	**Monterosso: Anchovy Festival**
June 18	**Monterosso and Vernazza: Feast of Corpus Domini** (procession on carpet of flowers)
June 24	**Riomaggiore and Monterosso: Feast day of St. John the Baptist** (procession and fireworks, floating candles on the sea; big fire on Monterosso's old town beach the day before)
June 29	**Corniglia: Feast day of Sts. Peter and Paul**
July 20	**Vernazza: Feast day of patron St. Margaret,** with fireworks
Early Aug (first Sun)	**Vernazza: Feast of Nostra Signora di Reggio** (hike up to Reggio Sanctuary for food and church procession)
Aug 10	**Manarola: Feast day of patron St. Lawrence**
Aug 15	**Feast of the Assumption** (Ferragosto)
Sept 8	**Monterosso: Feast of Madonna di Fegina** (luminarias and procession up to hilltop sanctuary)
Mid-Sept (third Sat)	**Monterosso: Anchovies and Olive Oil Festival**

Riomaggiore, one of the biggest Cinque Terre towns, has the cheapest beds and rivals Monterosso for nightlife, but it's more Italian than Rivieran, and its hoteliers can be flaky.

Corniglia, on a hilltop (no beach), attracts hermits, anarchists, wine lovers, and mountain goats.

The Cinque Terre is popular with Italians, Germans, French, and in-the-know Americans. Accommodations cost more and are packed on holidays; in May, June, and September; and on Fridays and Saturdays all summer. (With climate change, sweltering August is no longer considered the peak of peak season on this stretch of the Riviera.) During these busy periods, it's essential to reserve in advance.

Private Rooms for Rent *(Affittacamere):* Many accommodations in the Cinque Terre (especially in Vernazza) are *affittacamere,* or private rooms for rent. These range from simple bedrooms with shared baths, to fancy bedrooms with private baths, to comfortable apartments (often with small kitchens). You get a key and come and go as you like, typically rarely seeing your landlord. Plan on paying cash. If you must cancel an *affittacamere* reservation, do it as early as possible—since people renting rooms usually don't take deposits, they lose money if you don't show up.

Outside of peak times, you can land a double room on any day just by arriving in town (ideally by noon) and asking around at bars and restaurants. Most locals know someone who rents rooms. Many travelers enjoy the opportunity to shop around a bit and get the best price by bargaining.

Amenities: Breakfast is not included at most *affittacamere* and other simple accommodations. (Locals take breakfast about as seriously as flossing.) The basic, very Italian choice is simply to drop by a neighborhood bar for a cappuccino and a *cornetto* (croissant) or a piece of focaccia. Some pricier places include breakfast, but this often consists of a few paltry items (packaged croissants, yogurt, instant coffee) in a minifridge in your room.

While air-conditioning is essential in the summer elsewhere in Italy, in the breezy Cinque Terre you can generally manage fine without it. Expect thin walls (pack earplugs).

Near the Cinque Terre

Riviera towns typically have modern hotels with the usual amenities. The hotels aren't necessarily cheaper than the Cinque Terre, but they are more likely to have space. High season is July and August; prices go down in April-June and September-October, and are soft the rest of the year. Some hotels close off-season. Especially in peak season, some hoteliers want you to pay for half-pension (lunch or dinner).

EATING

To help you eat well on a budget, I've rated my recommended restaurants with a price code (see page 9). Below, I'll cover general tips, then offer advice specific to the Cinque Terre.

Tips on Eating in Italy

Restaurants generally serve lunch from 13:00 to 15:00 (and rarely open their doors before noon), and dinner from 19:00. Most kitchens close down between lunch and dinner.

A full Italian meal consists of several courses—an appetizer *(antipasto),* a first course *(primo piatto),* and a second course (*secondo piatto,* usually meat or seafood)—but no one is obliged to order all that food. To stretch your budget and avoid getting stuffed, you can share dishes. For example, a couple can order and share two *antipasti* and two *primi,* or whatever combination appeals.

Make sure you're clear on the price before ordering. Seafood and steak may be sold by weight (either priced by the kilo—1,000 grams, or just over two pounds; or by the *etto*—100 grams, about a quarter-pound). The abbreviation *s.q. (secondo quantità)* means an item is priced "according to quantity" (such as the size of a fish). Especially for steak, restaurants may require a minimum order of four or five *etti* (which diners can share). Some special dishes come in larger quantities meant to be shared by two people (you'll see "X2" on the menu), though the price listed generally indicates the cost per person.

To get a full meal at a predictable price, consider the *menu turistico*—a fixed-price multicourse meal (which you choose from a list of menu items). It includes the service charge, and is usually a good value for non-gourmets.

Only rude waiters rush you. You'll have to ask for the bill—mime-scribble on your raised palm or ask: *"Il conto?"*

Cover and Tipping: Before you sit down, look at a menu to see the extra charges a restaurant usually tacks on. The *coperto* (a.k.a. *pane e coperto*) is a non-negotiable cover charge, added onto your bill as a flat fee (usually €1-3.50 per person and noted on the menu). The *servizio* (service charge) of about 10 percent pays for the waitstaff. At most eateries, the words *servizio incluso* on the menu or bill mean that prices already include the fee. Most Italians don't tip beyond that. But if you want to tip extra, add €1-2 for each person in your party. This bonus amount usually comes out to about 5 percent (10 percent is excessive).

Budget Options: Try an Italian bar—an inexpensive café (open to kids, too) serving sandwiches, minipizzas, salads, coffee, and more. Many bars have a clearly posted two- or three-tiered pricing system. If you order, say, a sandwich, it's cheapest if you eat it standing at the bar, more if you sit at an indoor table, and the most at an outdoor table.

Picnicking saves euros. At a deli *(rosticceria),* takeout pizza shop, grocery, or open-air market, it's easy to assemble a delicious picnic.

On the Cinque Terre

Hanging out at a seaview restaurant while sampling local specialties could become one of your favorite memories.

The key staple is anchovies (*acciughe;* ah-CHOO-gay)—ideally served the day they're caught. If you've always hated anchovies (the slimy, salty kind), try them fresh here. They are prepared in a dizzying variety of ways: marinated, salted, drenched in lemon juice, butterflied and deep-fried (sometimes with a delicious garlic/vinegar sauce called *giada*), and so on.

Tegame alla vernazzana is the most typical main course in Vernazza: a layered, casserole-like dish of whole anchovies, potatoes, tomatoes, white wine, oil, and herbs.

Seafood is plentiful. You'll often see *muscoli ripieni* (stuffed mussels). And, while antipasto means cheese and salami in Tuscany, here you'll get *antipasti frutti di mare* (or simply *antipasti misti*): a plate of mixed "fruits of the sea." Many restaurants are proud of their *frutti di mare*—it's how they

Try the wonderfully fresh seafood and pesto pasta. Buon appetito!

show off—and it's a fine way to start a meal. For two diners, splitting one of these and a pasta dish can be plenty.

This region is the birthplace of pesto. Basil, which loves the temperate Ligurian climate, is ground with cheese (half parmigiano and half pecorino), garlic, olive oil, and pine nuts, and then poured over pasta. You'll see it on gnocchi or on pasta designed specifically for pesto to cling to: *trenette* (the long, flat Ligurian noodle ruffled on one side) or *trofie* (short, dense twists made of flour with a bit of potato). Many also like pesto lasagna, always made with white sauce, never red. If you become addicted, small jars of pesto are sold in grocery stores and gift shops.

Pansotti are ravioli with ricotta and a mixture of greens, often served with a walnut sauce *(salsa di noci)*...delightful and filling.

Focaccia—pillowy, flat, salty, olive-oily bread—also originates here in Liguria. The baker roughs up the dough with finger holes, sprinkles it with salt water, then bakes it. Focaccia comes plain or with onions, sage, or olives, and is a local favorite for a snack on the beach. Bakeries sell it in rounds or slices by weight (a portion is about 100 grams, or *un etto*).

Farinata, a humble flatbread snack sold at pizza and focaccia places, is made from chickpea flour, water, oil, and pepper and baked on a copper tray in a wood-burning stove. It's dense, filling, and less flavorful than focaccia.

The region also loves its locally grown lemons. The popular lemon liqueur is called limoncino (a.k.a. limoncello).

Vino delle Cinque Terre, while not one of Italy's top wines, flows cheap and easy throughout the region. It's white—crisp, refreshing, and great with seafood. Local wines are typically blends, predominantly using the bosco grape, found only here.

For a sweet dessert wine, *sciacchetrà* (shah-keh-TRAH) is worth the splurge (€4 per small glass, often served with dunkable cookies). You could order the fun dessert *torta della nonna* ("grandmother's cake") and dunk chunks of it into your glass. Aged *sciacchetrà* finishes dry and costs more (up to €12/glass). While 10 kilos of grapes yield 7 liters of local wine, *sciacchetrà* is made from near-raisins, and 10 kilos of grapes make only 1.5 liters of the wine. The word means "push and pull"—push in lots of grapes, pull out the best wine. If your room is up a lot of steps, be warned: *Sciacchetrà* is 18 percent alcohol, while regular wine is only 11 percent.

STAYING CONNECTED

You can bring your own mobile device (phone, tablet, laptop) and follow my budget tips. Or buy a European SIM card for your phone. Or just use European landlines and computers. These three options are described below (and in full at www.ricksteves.com/phoning). But first, here's the scoop on...

Making Calls

To **call Italy from the US or Canada:** Dial 011 (international access code), 39 (Italy's country code), and the local number.

To **call Italy from a European country:** Dial 00, then 39 followed by the local number.

To **make calls within Italy,** just dial the local number.

To **call from Italy to another country:** Dial 00, the country code (for example, 1 for the US or Canada), then the number.

Initial Zero: Drop the initial zero from the local number when calling internationally—except when calling Italy.

Mobile Tip: Pressing the + sign auto-selects the correct international access code.

Budget Tips for Using Your Mobile Device in Europe

Use free Wi-Fi whenever possible. Unless you have an unlimited data plan, save most of your online tasks for Wi-Fi. Many hotels and cafés have Wi-Fi for guests.

Sign up for an international plan. Most providers offer a global plan that cuts the cost of calls and texts, and gives you a block of data. Your normal plan may already include this coverage (T-Mobile's does).

Minimize the use of your cellular network. If you can't find Wi-Fi, you can roam on your cellular network. When you're done, avoid further charges by disabling "data roaming" or "cellular data" in your settings. Save bandwidth-gobbling tasks (Skyping, downloading apps, streaming) for when you're on Wi-Fi.

Use calling/messaging apps for cheaper calls and texts. Some apps (Skype, Viber, FaceTime, Google+ Hangouts) let you call or text for free or cheap.

Using a European SIM Card

This option helps you get faster data connections and make voice calls at cheap local rates. Either buy a basic phone in Europe (about $40 from mobile-phone shops) or bring an "unlocked" US phone. In Europe, buy a SIM card to insert in your phone, giving you a European phone number. Buy a new card when you arrive in a new country (sold at phone shops, newsstands, vending machines, and department-store electronics counters).

Using Landlines and Computers

If it's inexpensive to make calls from your **hotel-room phone** (ask at the desk for rates before you dial), you can make your calls even cheaper by using an **international phone card** *(carta telefonica prepagata internazionale;* sold at post offices, newsstands, street kiosks, and train stations). You'll get either a card with a toll-free number plus a PIN code, or just a code printed on a receipt.

Italy's few **public pay phones** work with an insertable Telecom Italia phone card, sold at post offices and newsstands.

You'll find **public computers** in Internet cafés and some hotel lobbies. On a European keyboard, use the "Alt Gr" key to type symbols (such as @) that appear on some keys.

RESOURCES FROM RICK STEVES

My website, **RickSteves.com,** offers a wealth of free travel information, including videos and podcasts of my shows and classes (www.ricksteves.com/travel-talks), travel forums, guidebook updates, my travel blog, and my guide to European rail passes—plus an **online travel store** and information on our many **tours of Europe** (www.ricksteves.com/tours).

This Pocket Guide is one of many **guidebooks** in my series on European travel, including guides to Italy and major Italian cities. I also produce a **public television series,** *Rick Steves' Europe* (see free episodes, including the Cinque Terre, at www.ricksteves.com/tv), and a **public radio show,** *Travel with Rick Steves.*

My free **Rick Steves Audio Europe App** makes it easy for you to download my audio tours of many of Europe's top attractions as well as insightful travel interviews with experts from around the globe (www.ricksteves.com/audioeurope).

Packing Checklist

Clothing

- ❑ 5 shirts: long- & short-sleeve
- ❑ 2 pairs pants (or skirts/capris)
- ❑ 1 pair shorts
- ❑ 5 pairs underwear & socks
- ❑ 1 pair walking shoes
- ❑ Sweater or warm layer
- ❑ Rainproof jacket with hood
- ❑ Tie, scarf, belt, and/or hat
- ❑ Swimsuit
- ❑ Sleepwear/loungewear

Money

- ❑ Debit/credit card(s)
- ❑ Hard cash ($100-200 in US dollars)
- ❑ Money belt

Documents

- ❑ Passport
- ❑ Tickets & confirmations: flights, hotels, trains, rail pass, car rental, sight entries
- ❑ Driver's license
- ❑ Student ID, hostel card, etc.
- ❑ Photocopies of important docs.
- ❑ Insurance details
- ❑ Guidebooks & maps
- ❑ Notepad & pen
- ❑ Journal

Toiletries Kit

- ❑ Soap, shampoo, toothbrush/paste, deodorant, sunscreen, brush/comb
- ❑ Medicines & vitamins
- ❑ First-aid kit
- ❑ Glasses/contacts/sunglasses
- ❑ Sewing kit
- ❑ Packet of tissues (for WC)
- ❑ Earplugs

Electronics

- ❑ Mobile phone
- ❑ Camera & related gear
- ❑ Tablet/ebook reader/laptop
- ❑ Headphones
- ❑ Chargers & batteries
- ❑ Smartphone car charger & mount (or GPS device)
- ❑ Plug adapters

Miscellaneous

- ❑ Daypack
- ❑ Sealable plastic baggies
- ❑ Laundry supplies
- ❑ Small umbrella
- ❑ Travel alarm/watch

Optional Extras

- ❑ Second pair of shoes
- ❑ Travel hairdryer
- ❑ Picnic supplies
- ❑ Water bottle
- ❑ Fold-up tote bag
- ❑ Small flashlight
- ❑ Mini binoculars
- ❑ Small towel or washcloth
- ❑ Inflatable pillow/neck rest
- ❑ Tiny lock
- ❑ Extra passport photos

Italian Survival Phrases

Good day.	**Buon giorno.**	bwohn JOR-noh
Mr. / Mrs.	**Signore / Signora**	seen-YOH-ray / seen-YOH-rah
Miss	**Signorina**	seen-yoh-REE-nah
Do you speak English?	**Parla inglese?**	PAR-lah een-GLEH-zay
Yes. / No.	**Si. / No.**	see / noh
I (don't) understand.	**(Non) capisco.**	(nohn) kah-PEES-koh
Please.	**Per favore.**	pehr fah-VOH-ray
Thank you.	**Grazie.**	GRAHT-see-ay
You're welcome.	**Prego.**	PREH-go
I'm sorry.	**Mi dispiace.**	mee dee-spee-AH-chay
Excuse me.	**Mi scusi.**	mee SKOO-zee
(No) problem.	**(Non) c'è un problema.**	(nohn) cheh oon proh-BLEH-mah
Good.	**Va bene.**	vah BEH-nay
Goodbye.	**Arrivederci.**	ah-ree-veh-DEHR-chee
one / two	**uno / due**	OO-noh / DOO-ay
three / four	**tre / quattro**	tray / KWAH-troh
five / six	**cinque / sei**	CHEEN-kway / SEH-ee
seven / eight	**sette / otto**	SEH-tay / OH-toh
nine / ten	**nove / dieci**	NOH-vay / dee-AY-chee
How much is it?	**Quanto costa?**	KWAHN-toh KOH-stah
Is it free?	**È gratis?**	eh GRAH-tees
Is it included?	**È incluso?**	eh een-KLOO-zoh
Can you help me?	**Può aiutarmi?**	pwoh ah-yoo-TAR-mee
Where can I buy / find...?	**Dove posso comprare / trovare...?**	DOH-vay POH-soh kohm-PRAH-ray / troh-VAH-ray
I'd like / We'd like...	**Vorrei / Vorremmo...**	voh-REH-ee / voh-REH-moh
...a room.	**...una camera.**	OO-nah KAH-meh-rah
...a ticket to ___.	**...un biglietto per ___.**	oon beel-YEH-toh pehr ___
Is it possible?	**È possibile?**	eh poh-SEE-bee-lay
Where is...?	**Dov'è...?**	doh-VEH
...tourist information	**...informazioni per turisti**	een-for-maht-see-OH-nee pehr too-REE-stee
...a cash machine	**...un bancomat**	oon BAHN-koh-maht
...the toilet	**...la toilette**	lah twah-LEH-tay
men	**uomini / signori**	WOH-mee-nee / seen-YOH-ree
women	**donne / signore**	DOH-nay / seen-YOH-ray
left / right	**sinistra / destra**	see-NEE-strah / DEH-strah
straight	**sempre dritto**	SEHM-pray DREE-toh
When does this open / close?	**A che ora apre / chiude?**	ah kay OH-rah AH-pray / kee-OO-day
At what time?	**A che ora?**	ah kay OH-rah
Just a moment.	**Un momento.**	oon moh-MEHN-toh
now / soon / later	**adesso / presto / tardi**	ah-DEH-soh / PREH-stoh / TAR-dee
today / tomorrow	**oggi / domani**	OH-jee / doh-MAH-nee

In the Restaurant

I'd like / We'd like...	**Vorrei / Vorremmo...**	voh-REH-ee / vor-REH-moh
...to reserve...	**...prenotare...**	preh-noh-TAH-ray
...a table for one / two.	**...un tavolo per uno / due.**	oon TAH-voh-loh pehr OO-noh / DOO-ay
Is this table free?	**È libero questo tavolo?**	eh LEE-beh-roh KWEH-stoh TAH-voh-loh
The menu (in English), please.	**Il menù (in inglese), per favore.**	eel may-NOO (een een-GLEH-zay) pehr fah-VOH-ray
breakfast	**colazione**	koh-laht-see-OH-nay
lunch	**pranzo**	PRAHNT-soh
dinner	**cena**	CHEH-nah
service (not) included	**servizio (non) incluso**	sehr-VEET-see-oh (nohn) een-KLOO-zoh
cover charge	**pane e coperto**	PAH-nay ay koh-PEHR-toh
to go	**da portar via**	dah por-TAR VEE-ah
menu (of the day)	**menù (del giorno)**	may-NOO (dehl JOR-noh)
specialty of the house	**specialità della casa**	speh-chah-lee-TAH DEH-lah KAH-zah
first course (pasta, soup)	**primo piatto**	PREE-moh pee-AH-toh
main course (meat, fish)	**secondo piatto**	seh-KOHN-doh pee-AH-toh
side dishes	**contorni**	kohn-TOR-nee
bread / cheese	**pane / formaggio**	PAH-nay / for-MAH-joh
sandwich	**panino**	pah-NEE-noh
soup / salad	**zuppa / insalata**	TSOO-pah / een-sah-LAH-tah
meat	**carni**	KAR-nee
chicken	**pollo**	POH-loh
fish	**pesce**	PEH-shay
seafood	**frutti di mare**	FROO-tee dee MAH-ray
dessert	**dolce**	DOHL-chay
tap water	**acqua del rubinetto**	AH-kwah dehl roo-bee-NEH-toh
mineral water	**acqua minerale**	AH-kwah mee-neh-RAH-lay
milk	**latte**	LAH-tay
(orange) juice	**succo (d'arancia)**	SOO-koh (dah-RAHN-chah)
coffee / tea	**caffè / tè**	kah-FEH / teh
wine	**vino**	VEE-noh
red / white	**rosso / bianco**	ROH-soh / bee-AHN-koh
glass / bottle	**bicchiere / bottiglia**	bee-kee-EH-ray / boh-TEEL-yah
beer	**birra**	BEE-rah
Cheers!	**Cin cin!**	cheen cheen
More. / Another.	**Di più. / Un altro.**	dee pew / oon AHL-troh
The same.	**Lo stesso.**	loh STEH-soh
The bill, please.	**Il conto, per favore.**	eel KOHN-toh pehr fah-VOH-ray
Do you accept credit cards?	**Accettate carte di credito?**	ah-cheh-TAH-tay KAR-tay dee KREH-dee-toh
tip	**mancia**	MAHN-chah
Delicious!	**Delizioso!**	day-leet-see-OH-zoh

For more user-friendly Italian phrases, check out *Rick Steves' Italian Phrase Book & Dictionary* or *Rick Steves' French, Italian, and German Phrase Book.*

INDEX

Index

D

E

F

R

S

T

V

PHOTO CREDITS

Title Page
© Dominic Arizona Bonuccelli

TOC
Left: © Dominic Arizona Bonuccelli, right: © Rick Steves

Page 4 © birillo81/123rf.com

Page 108 © iryna1/123rf.com

Additional photography by: Dominic Arizona Bonuccelli, Cameron Hewitt, Heather Locke, Gene Openshaw, Paul Orcutt, Rick Steves, Laura VanDeventer and Ragen Van Sewell. Photos used are by permission and are property of the original copyright holder.

ricksteves.com

your travel dreams into affordable reality

Radio Interviews

Enjoy ready access to Rick's vast library of radio interviews covering travel tips and cultural insights that relate specifically to your Europe travel plans.

Travel Forums

Learn, ask, share! Our online community of savvy travelers is a great resource for first-time travelers to Europe, as well as seasoned pros. You'll find forums on each country, plus travel tips and restaurant/hotel reviews. You can even ask one of our well-traveled staff to chime in with an opinion.

Travel News

Subscribe to our free Travel News e-newsletter, and get monthly updates from Rick on what's happening in Europe.

Pack Light and Right

Gear up for your next adventure at ricksteves.com

Light Luggage

Pack light and right with Rick Steves' affordable, custom-designed rolling carry-on bags, backpacks, day packs and shoulder bags.

Accessories

From packing cubes to moneybelts and beyond, Rick has personally selected the travel goodies that will help your trip go smoother.

Shop at ricksteves.com

Rick Steves has

Experience maximum Europe

Save time and energy

This guidebook is your independent-travel toolkit. But for all it delivers, it's still up to you to devote the time and energy it takes to manage the preparation and logistics that are essential for a happy trip. If that's a hassle, there's a solution.

Rick Steves Tours

A Rick Steves tour takes you to Europe's most interesting places with great guides and small groups

great tours, too!

with minimum stress

of 28 or less. We follow Rick's favorite itineraries, ride in comfy buses, stay in family-run hotels, and bring you intimately close to the Europe you've traveled so far to see. Most importantly, we take away the logistical headaches so you can focus on the fun.

Join the fun

This year we'll take thousands of free-spirited travelers—nearly half

of them repeat customers—along with us on four dozen different itineraries, from Ireland to Italy to Istanbul. Is a Rick Steves tour the right fit for your travel dreams? Find out at ricksteves.com, where you can also request Rick's latest tour catalog.

Europe is best experienced with happy travel partners. We hope you can join us.

See our itineraries at ricksteves.com

Rick Steves®

BEST OF GUIDES

Best of England
Best of France
Best of Germany
Best of Ireland
Best of Italy
Best of Spain

EUROPE GUIDES

Best of Europe
Eastern Europe
Europe Through the Back Door
Mediterranean Cruise Ports
Northern European Cruise Ports

COUNTRY GUIDES

Croatia & Slovenia
England
France
Germany
Great Britain
Ireland
Italy
Portugal
Scandinavia
Scotland
Spain
Switzerland

CITY & REGIONAL GUIDES

Amsterdam & the Netherlands
Belgium: Bruges, Brussels, Antwerp & Ghent
Barcelona
Budapest
Florence & Tuscany
Greece: Athens & the Peloponnese
Istanbul
London
Paris
Prague & the Czech Republic
Provence & the French Riviera
Rome
Venice
Vienna, Salzburg & Tirol

SNAPSHOT GUIDES

Basque Country: Spain & France
Berlin
Copenhagen & the Best of Denmark
Dublin
Dubrovnik
Hill Towns of Central Italy
Krakow, Warsaw & Gdansk
Lisbon
Loire Valley
Madrid & Toledo

Nearly all Rick Steves guides are available as ebooks. Check with your favorite bookseller.

Rick Steves guidebooks are published by Avalon Travel, an imprint of Perseus Books, a Hachette Book Group company.

Maximize your travel skills with a good guidebook.

Milan & the Italian Lakes District
Naples & the Amalfi Coast
Northern Ireland
Norway
Sevilla, Granada & Southern Spain
St. Petersburg, Helsinki & Tallinn
Stockholm

POCKET GUIDES

Amsterdam
Athens
Barcelona
Florence
Italy's Cinque Terre
London
Munich & Salzburg
Paris
Prague
Rome
Venice
Vienna

TRAVEL CULTURE

Europe 101
European Christmas
Postcards from Europe
Travel as a Political Act

***RICK STEVES' EUROPE* DVDs**

12 New Shows 2015-2016
Austria & the Alps
The Complete Collection 2000-2016
Eastern Europe
England & Wales
European Christmas
European Travel Skills & Specials
France
Germany, BeNeLux & More
Greece, Turkey & Portugal
The Holy Land: Israelis & Palestinians Today
Iran
Ireland & Scotland
Italy's Cities
Italy's Countryside
Scandinavia
Spain
Travel Extras

PHRASE BOOKS & DICTIONARIES

French
French, Italian & German
German
Italian
Portuguese
Spanish

PLANNING MAPS

Britain, Ireland & London
Europe
France & Paris
Germany, Austria & Switzerland
Ireland
Italy
Spain & Portugal

RickSteves.com **@RickSteves**

Rick Steves books are available at bookstores
and through online booksellers.